ST. JOSEPH'S TREASURY

A MANUAL OF DEVOTIONAL PRAYERS

ST. JOSEPH'S TREASURY

A MANUAL OF DEVOTIONAL PRAYERS

Fr. Michael A. Odubela, OSJ

ST. JOSEPH'S TREASURY MANUAL OF
DEVOTIONAL PRAYERS

ISBN: 978-978-785-038-1

Year of Publication 2023
Reprint 2024

Imprimatur: Fr. Paul Agabo, OSJ
Provincial,
Our Lady Queen of Nigeria Province,
Oblates of St. Joseph.
June 1, 2023

Cover Image: Taken directly from a Holy Family
Statue in the General Council's meeting Rome.
Statue maker is unknown

Printed by:
Totma O Prints Enterprise, Lagos
Tel: 08026307564

CONTENT

I hope that this book will help us draw closer to Jesus, to make Him known, loved and served better through the promotion of devotion to Saint Joseph, Husband of Mary and father of Jesus.

FOREWORD

Without question, the Immaculate Virgin Mary, Mother of God, is the greatest of all Saints and the most powerful intercessor of all. Next to her, in a manner also unequaled by any other Saint, is St. Joseph, her most Holy Spouse, the Just Man of the line of David, chosen for and with her to receive the Son of God Incarnate into this world. Together they raised Him and lived in the Holy Family with Him for 30 years. He who was closest to Jesus and Mary on earth and certainly remains closest to Him in Heaven.

Although devotion to St. Joseph has developed slowly through the centuries, it has flourished in recent centuries, and most especially during the most recent decades. As an Oblate of St. Joseph, Fr. Michael Odubela has dedicated his life to imitating St. Joseph and leading others to do the same. He has collected in this *Manual* a very extensive *Treasury* of devotions to him to be shared with all of you. In addition to St. Joseph's principal roles as Husband of Mary, earthly father of Jesus, and Patron of the Church, you will find herein a wealth of his many other titles and patronages. Prayers for so many various needs and graces show that St. Joseph is a truly universal patron for every situation. Using these daily prayers, Wednesday devotions, and various novenas will certainly help you to grow in holiness. Preparing for and consecrating yourself to St. Joseph will truly help you be a member of the Holy Family.

Fr. Larry Toschi, OSJ

PROMOTION OF DEVOTION TO ST. JOSEPH

The need to promote devotion to St. Joseph has become more urgent now than ever before with the various forms of desecration of human life, family life and values. The abasement and debasement of the father figure in families and the erosion of authentic alpha role models in the society make the need for a true father figure indispensable. Every family needs a head who is an exemplary role model, a respecter of life, and an accountable steward, whom the Lord is pleased to place in charge of His household to watch over it in the example of His own Fatherly love.

For those who do not know St. Joseph yet, be sure that you are not alone in your ignorance as regards our noble Saint as even St. John of the Cross was once in that situation and he confessed: "I did not understand him [St. Joseph] well enough, but that will change". Yes, you too can bring about the needed change and *Ite ad Ioseph* (Go to Joseph)! Those who already know St. Joseph have the responsibility to make him known to many others who do not yet know him, just as St. Theresa of Avila did to St. John of the Cross. So in love, in prayers, in virtue and in zeal, let us promote the glories of St. Joseph and spread devotion to him everywhere we go and to everyone we know or encounter. Take all to St. Joseph, that they may be in better relationship with Jesus and Mary.

Pope Francis made it clear in the concluding part of the *Patris Corde* that the "aim of this Apostolic Letter is to increase our love for this great saint, to encourage us to implore his intercession and to imitate his virtues and his zeal". Thus, we are invited to improve our relationship with St. Joseph, take him as our spiritual father, ask for help and blessings through him, and model ourselves after the example of his virtuous living and zeal for the Lord's service as did several saints before us.

We should thus strive to develop a Christ-centred devotion to St. Joseph, not only in his role as Husband of Mary and father of Jesus, as contained in the Sacred Scriptures, but also in his life and role in the mystery of salvation. Such devotion will lead us to a deeper contemplation of the glories of God, the cultivation of daily virtuous living and constant recourse to the intercession of St. Joseph. It will strengthen the drive to promote healthy family life among spouses and among their children, so that the family bond increases, and the value of chastity and filial obedience are all the more appreciated. It will also make the devotion easy to understand and practice by every member of the faithful.

It is my hope that we grow in prayer with a heart like Joseph's - a heart so gentle, pure and loving. I wish to recommend this book to all who truly desire to draw closer to God and serve Him in "imitation of St. Joseph", a faithful and true servant of the divine mysteries.

Therefore, beloved in Christ, let us pay heed as Blessed Pope Pius IX reminds us that "In Joseph … heads of the household are blessed with the unsurpassed model of fatherly watchfulness and care." He encourages us to "Go to Joseph! Have recourse with special confidence to St. Joseph, for his protection is most powerful, as he is the Patron of the Universal Church."

Ite ad Ioseph!

FOLLOWING THE FOOTSTEPS OF SAINTS

"God sets a father in honour over his children…" (Sirach 3:2)

St. Joseph was declared Patron of the Universal Church by Pope Pius IX in 1870. He was officially entrusted with the care of the Church by the Vicar of Christ, so that he watches over her as he did the Holy Family's home in Nazareth. St. John Paul II stated this when he said, "Inspired by the Gospel, the Fathers of the Church from the earliest centuries stressed that just as St. Joseph took loving care of Mary and gladly dedicated himself to Jesus Christ's upbringing, he likewise watches over and protects Christ's Mystical Body, that is, the Church, of which the Virgin Mary is the exemplar and model."

The importance is further appreciated when Pope Francis, on celebrating the 150 years of the declaration of St. Joseph as Patron of the Universal Church declared a Year of St. Joseph on December 8, 2020. The declaration was accompanied by an Apostolic Letter *Patris Corde* through which the Holy Father sets forth some teachings on the life of St. Joseph, in relation to family life and with particular attention to the role of a father in the family. He built on the Josephology of previous Popes and strikingly made clear that the greatness of St. Joseph is rooted in his role as "the spouse of Mary and the father of Jesus" *(PC. 1).*

In her autobiography, the holy Carmelite mystic and reformer St. Theresa of Avila sings the praises of her holy father, St. Joseph, and gives proof of his powerful intercession:

"I took for my patron and lord the glorious St. Joseph, and recommended myself earnestly to him. I saw clearly that both out of this my present trouble, and out of others of greater importance, relating to my honour and the loss of my soul, this my father and lord delivered me, and rendered me greater services than I knew how to ask for."

St. Theresa was a faithful and convinced devotee in this regard. She did not only personally experience the power of intercession of St. Joseph; she also proclaimed the same and recommended souls to his care and intercession. Her confidence and trust in St. Joseph stems from her personal experience: "It is now very many years since I began asking him for something on his feast, and I always received it. If the petition was in any way amiss, he rectified it for my greater good." "I know by experience that the glorious St. Joseph assists us generally in all necessities. I never asked him for anything which he did not obtain for me"; and so she recommends to others: "Knowing by experience St. Joseph's astonishing influence with God, I would wish to persuade everyone to honour him with particular devotion. I have always seen those who honored him in a special manner make progress in virtue, for this heavenly protector favours in a striking manner the spiritual advancement of souls who commend themselves to him".

She also makes clear that the best reason to love and to have recourse to St. Joseph is because Jesus and Mary did so!

St. Joseph Marello, founder of the Oblates of St. Joseph (OSJ) who was also confident in the same protective and intercessory power of St. Joseph, the Guardian of the Redeemer, teaches his sons "To serve the interest of Jesus, like St. Joseph" and to always say to him:

"Here we are, all for you, and you be all for us, O Joseph, teach us the way, guide our every step, lead us where Divine Providence wants us to be. Whether the journey is long or short, smooth or rough, whether the goal is within the range of human sight or not, whether our pace is fast or slow, with you, O Joseph, we are sure to always go well".

Assured of the consistent help of St. Joseph, he would say, "If St. Joseph did not grant graces, he would not be St. Joseph". He reminds us that "St. Joseph did not do extraordinary things, but rather by the constant practice of ordinary and common virtues, he attained that sanctity which elevates him above all the other saints."

St. Faustina Kowalska (*Diary of St. Faustina*, 1203) also highlights the role of the Nurturing Father of Jesus in drawing souls to the merciful Heart of God: "St. Joseph urged me to have a constant devotion to

him. He himself told me to recite three prayers [the Our Father, Hail Mary, and Glory be and the Memorare once every day. He looked at me with great kindness and made me know how much he is supporting this work [of mercy]. He has promised me this special help and protection. I recite the requested prayers every day and feel his special protection." The Memorare prayer referred to by St. Faustina is the 'Memorare to St. Joseph' that her Congregation prayed each day.

St. Peter Julian Eymard was utterly certain of the power of St, Joseph's intercession and his life as being relatable and so encourages us that "Devotion to St. Joseph is one of the choicest graces that God can give to a soul, for it is tantamount to revealing the entire treasury of our Lord's graces. When God wishes to raise a soul to greater heights, he unites it to St. Joseph by giving it a strong love for the good saint". He said that "a perfect imitation of St. Joseph is the best way to serve the interest of Jesus". He reminds us that "He [St. Joseph] is patron of vocations, so pray to him for the grace of fulfilling your duties well and of directing your children in their path of life. Inspire them with devotion to St. Joseph. It will bring them happiness." He further encourages "Make him [St. Joseph] the patron of your family and you will soon have tangible proof of his protecting hand". He reminds us that "St. Joseph is our guide and our model. Because our vocation is like his, we must live his life, practice his virtues, and assimilate his spirit".

Venerable Margaret of the Most Holy Sacrament, a holy Carmelite nun, known endearingly as the "Spouse of His Holy Infancy," loved to meditate on the Childhood of Jesus and His life with Mary and Joseph. By her own example of love and devotion, she encourages all Christians to venerate St. Joseph as the worthy spouse of the Mother of God and the guardian of the "Immaculate Word".

St. Josemaria Escriva, spoke of Joseph's active faith, "He kept the commandments of God without wavering, even though the meaning of those commandments was sometimes obscure or their relation to the rest of the divine plan hidden from him… Joseph's faith does not falter, he obeys quickly and to the letter". He reminds us that "Saint Joseph, our father and lord, is a teacher of the interior life. Place yourself under his patronage and you'll feel the effectiveness of his power." He convincingly says, "One cannot love Jesus and Mary without loving the Holy Patriarch."

DAILY DEVOTIONS TO ST. JOSEPH

Morning Offering to St. Joseph

Receive me, dear and chosen father, glorious St. Joseph, and the offering of every movement of my body and soul, which I desire to present through thee to my blessed Lord. Purify all! Make all a perfect holocaust! May every pulsation of my heart be a Spiritual Communion, every look and thought an act of love, every action a sweet sacrifice, every word an arrow of Divine love, every step an advance towards Jesus, every visit to Our Lord as pleasing to God as the errands of Angels, every thought of thee, dear Saint, an act to remind thee that I am thy child. I recommend to thee the occasions in which I usually fail, particularly (*Mention those occasions and your habitual sins*). Accept each little devotion of the day, though replete with imperfection, and offer it to Jesus, whose mercy will overlook all, since He regards not so much the gift as the love of the giver. Amen.

Daily Act of Consecration to St. Joseph

O dearest St. Joseph, I consecrate myself to your honour and give myself to you that you may always be my father, my protector, and my guide in the way of salvation. Obtain for me a greater purity of heart and a fervent love of the interior life. After your example, may I do all my actions for the greater glory of God, in union with the Sacred Heart of Jesus and the Immaculate Heart of Mary. O Blessed St. Joseph, pray for me that I may share in the peace and joy of your holy death. Amen.

Memorare to St. Joseph

Remember, O most chaste spouse of the Virgin Mary, that never was it known that anyone who fled to your protection, implored your help, or sought your intercession was left unassisted. Full of confidence in your power, I fly unto you and beg your protection. Despise not, O Guardian of the Redeemer, my humble supplication, but in your bounty, hear and answer me. Amen.

Memorare to Mary and Joseph

Remember O Most Gracious Virgin Mary and St. Joseph that never was it known that anyone who fled to your protection, implored your help, or sought your intercession was left unaided. Inspired by this confidence, I come to you, O Virgin of Virgins, my mother, and you, Minister of Salvation, my spiritual father, sinful and sorrowful, O Mother of the Word Incarnate and you Guardian of the Redeemer despise not my petitions, but in your goodness and bounty, hear and answer me. Amen.

Beautiful Old Prayer to St. Joseph

O Saint Joseph, whose protection is so great, so strong, so prompt before the throne of God, I place

in you all my interests and desires. O Saint Joseph, do assist me by your powerful intercession and obtain for me from your divine Son, our Lord Jesus Christ, all spiritual blessings, so that having experienced here below your heavenly power, I may offer my thanksgiving and homage to the most loving of fathers. O Saint Joseph, I never weary of contemplating you and Jesus asleep in your arms. I dare not approach while He reposes near your heart. Hold Him close in my name and kiss His fine head for me, and ask Him to return the kiss when I draw my dying breath. St. Joseph, patron of departing souls, pray for me. Amen.

<u>Heart of Joseph Prayer</u> (As found in the *The Life of Saint Joseph* by Blessed Maria Cecilia Baij)

O my God! How poorly do I respond to Your immense goodness, consideration and love! Consider me as entirely Yours. Make out of me whatever will be most pleasing to You. I have nothing to give You except my very being and every moment of my existence, and I wish to renew my complete gift of myself to You. Moreover, if I had the power to dispose of the hearts of all creatures, I would offer them all to You, and dedicate them all to Your love. Oh infinite, immeasurable, inexpressible, incomprehensible God! Accept this meagre offering of Your lowly servant Joseph (*you can supply your name to personalise the prayer*), who wishes to give himself entirely to You out of love.

Prayer to Sleeping St. Joseph to obtain Favours

Oh Saint Joseph, You are a man greatly favoured by the Most High. The angel of the Lord appeared to you in dreams, while you slept, to warn you and guide you as you cared for the Holy Family. You were both silent and strong, a loyal and courageous protector.

Dear Saint Joseph, as you rest in the Lord, confident of His absolute power and goodness, look upon me. Please take my need (mention your request here) into your heart, dream of it, and present it to your Son. Help me then, good Saint Joseph, to hear the voice of God, to arise, and act with love. I praise and thank God with joy. Saint Joseph, I love you. Amen.

Prayer to St. Joseph before Mass (For Priests)

O Blessed Joseph, happy man, to whom it was given not only to see and to hear that God Whom many kings longed to see, and saw not, to hear, and heard not; but also to carry Him in your arms, to embrace Him, to clothe Him, and guard and defend Him.

V. Pray for us, O Blessed Joseph.

R. That we may be made worthy of the promises of Christ.

O God, Who has given us a royal priesthood, we beseech Thee, that as Blessed Joseph was found worthy to touch with his hands, and to bear in his arms, Thy only-begotten Son, born of the Virgin

Mary, so may we be made fit, by cleanness of heart and blamelessness of life, to minister at Thy holy altar; may we, this day, with reverent devotion partake of the Sacred Body and Blood of Your Only-begotten Son, and may we in the world to come be accounted worthy of receiving an everlasting reward. Through the same Christ our Lord. Amen.

Prayer to St. Joseph After Mass (Also Prayer For Chastity)

O St. Joseph, father and guardian of virgins, to whose faithful custody Jesus Christ, innocence itself, and Mary, Virgin of virgins, were entrusted, I pray and beseech you, by each of these most dear pledges, Jesus and Mary, that being preserved from all uncleanness, I may with spotless mind, pure heart, and chaste body, serve Jesus and Mary most chastely all the days of my life. Amen.

Pope Francis' Prayer to St. Joseph (1) (From *Patris Corde*)

Hail, Guardian of the Redeemer, Spouse of the Blessed Virgin Mary, to you God entrusted his only Son; in you Mary placed her trust; with you Christ became man. Blessed Joseph, to us too, show yourself a father and guide us in the path of life. Obtain for us grace, mercy, and courage, and defend us from every evil. Amen.

Pope Francis' Prayer to St. Joseph (2)

(Recommended by Pope Francis, see foot note, *Patris Corde*)

Glorious Patriarch Saint Joseph, whose power makes the impossible possible, come to my aid in these times of anguish and difficulty. Take under your protection the serious and troubling situations that I commend to you, that they may have a happy outcome. My beloved father, all my trust is in you. Let it not be said that I invoked you in vain, and since you can do everything with Jesus and Mary, show me that your goodness is as great as your power. Amen

St. Louis Marie de Montfort's Prayer to St. Joseph

Hail Joseph the just, Wisdom is with you; blessed are you among all men and blessed is Jesus, the fruit of Mary, your faithful spouse. Holy Joseph, worthy nurturer-father of Jesus Christ, pray for us sinners and obtain divine Wisdom for us from God, now and at the hour of our death. Amen.

Prayer to St. Joseph by St. Francis de Sales

Glorious St. Joseph, Spouse of Mary, grant us, we beseech thee, thy paternal protection, through the Heart of Jesus Christ. O Thou whose infinite power reaches out to all our needs, rendering possible for us that which is impossible, look upon the concerns of thy children with fatherly countenance. In the troubles and sorrows that afflict us, we have confident recourse to thee. Deign to take under thy loving protection this important and difficult endeavor, the cause of our worries, and dispose its success to the glory of God and to the benefit of His faithful servants. Amen.

St. Joseph Marello's Prayer to St. Joseph

Here we are, all for you, and you be all for us, O Joseph, teach us the way, guide our every step, lead us where Divine Providence wants us to arrive. Whether the journey is long or short, smooth or rough, whether the goal is within the range of human sight or not, whether our pace is fast or slow, with you, O Joseph, we are sure to always go well. Amen!

Litany of St. Joseph

Lord, have mercy.	Lord, have mercy.
Christ, have mercy.	Christ, have mercy.
Lord, have mercy.	Lord, have mercy.
Christ, hear us.	Christ, graciously hear us.
God, the Father of Heaven,	Have mercy on us.
God, the Son, Redeemer of the world,	Have mercy on us.
God, the Holy Spirit,	Have mercy on us.
Holy Trinity, One God,	Have mercy on us.
Holy Mary,	pray for us.
St. Joseph,	pray for us.
Noble son of David,	pray for us.

Light of Patriarchs,	pray for us.
Husband of the Mother of God,	pray for us.
Guardian of the Redeemer	pray for us.
Chaste Guardian of the Virgin	pray for us.
Nurturer of the Son of God	pray for us.
Zealous Defender of Christ	pray for us.
Servant of Christ	pray for us
Minister of Salvation	pray for us.
Head of the Holy Family	pray for us.
Joseph most just	pray for us.
Joseph most chaste	pray for us.
Joseph most prudent	pray for us.
Joseph most brave	pray for us.
Joseph most obedient	pray for us.
Joseph most faithful	pray for us.
Mirror of patience	pray for us.
Lover of poverty	pray for us.
Model of Workers	pray for us.
Glory of Family Life	pray for us.
Guardian of Virgins	pray for us.
Pillar of families	pray for us.
Support in difficulties	pray for us.
Comfort of the Troubled	pray for us.
Hope of the Sick	pray for us.
Patron of Exiles	pray for us.
Patron of the Afflicted	pray for us.

Patron of the Poor   pray for us.

Patron of the Dying   pray for us.

Terror of demons   pray for us.

Protector of Holy Church,   pray for us.

Lamb of God, who takes away the sins of the world, spare us, O Lord.

Lamb of God, who takes away the sins of the world, graciously hear us, O Lord.

Lamb of God, who takes away the sins of the world, have mercy on us

He made him the lord of his household

- And prince over all his possessions.

Let us Pray:

O God, in your ineffable providence you were pleased to choose Blessed Joseph to be the husband of your most holy Mother; grant, we beg you, that we may be worthy to have him for our intercessor in heaven whom on earth we venerate as our Protector: You who live and reign forever and ever. Amen.

Pious Invocations (Ejaculatory Prayers)

Pious invocations or ejaculatory prayers are ways of fulfilling the Biblical call to "pray without ceasing." *(1 Thess. 5:18)*. These pious invocations to Saint

Joseph can help recall our minds and hearts to God as we go about our daily activities, and also help us stay connected with the Lord all day. Keep one in mind, at a time, and repeat it throughout the course of the day.

1. Jesus, Mary, and Joseph, I love you, save souls.

2. Jesus, Mary, and Joseph, I give you my heart and my soul. Jesus, Mary, and Joseph, assist me in my last agony. Jesus, Mary, and Joseph, may I breathe forth my soul in peace with you.

3. Jesus, Mary, and Joseph, may my soul send forth its last sigh in peace, with you to aid me.

4. Jesus, Mary and Joseph, watch over our family and keep us always in true peace and love.

5. Jesus, Mary, and Joseph, protect and save the unborn.

6. St. Joseph, model and patron of those who love the Sacred Heart of Jesus and the Immaculate Heart of Mary, pray for us.

7. Chaste Heart of Joseph, pray for us!

8. Help us, St. Joseph, in our earthly strife; ever to lead a pure and blameless life.

9. St. Joseph, beloved father of our Lord Jesus Christ, and true spouse of Mary ever Virgin, pray for us.

10. St. Joseph, our guide, watch over us and protect the Holy Church.

11. St. Joseph, saviour of the Saviour, defend us and save us from every danger.

12. St. Joseph our protector, pray for us.

13. St. Joseph, perfect adorer of Jesus, teach us reverence and true love for the Eucharist.

14. St. Joseph, husband of Mary, bless all Christian couples and make them models of sincere love and exemplary parents.

15. St. Joseph, guardian of children and youth, keep unfailing watch over our children, and protect them from all harm.

16. Grant, O holy Joseph, that, ever secure under your protection, we may pass our lives without guilt.

17. St. Joseph, terror of demons, ward off from us the assaults of the evil one.

18. St. Joseph most just, help us to respect the rights of others and be just in our dealings today.

St. Alphonsus Liguori's Daily Devotion to St. Joseph

Adapted by Hugh J. O'Connell, C.Ss.R.

PRAYER FOR EACH DAY

Read the reflection proper to the day and then close each day with this follow up prayer

Most holy Patriarch, St. Joseph, I rejoice at the great dignity to which thou hast been raised in being made

nurturer father of the Son of God, endowed with authority to command Him Whom heaven and earth obey. My holy patron, since Jesus Himself respected and served thee as His father, I, too, wish to enroll myself in thy service. I choose thee, after Mary, for my principal advocate and protector. I promise to honour thee every day with some special devotion, and each day I will place myself under thy protection. As thou didst enjoy the sweet company of Jesus and Mary during thy life on earth, grant that I may ever live close to them and never be separated from God by losing His grace. And as thou wert assisted by Jesus and Mary at the hour of thy death, so grant me protection at the hour of my death, that, dying in thy presence and that of Jesus and Mary, I may one day go to thank thee in paradise, and in thy company praise and love God for all eternity. Amen.

**St. Joseph, patron of the universal Church, protect us. Protect our Holy Father, the Pope, and our Mother, Holy Church.*

FIRST DAY

God, because of the great love He bears us, and His great desire to see us saved, has given us among other means of salvation the practice of devotion to the saints. It is His will that they, who are His friends, should intercede for us, and by their merits and prayers obtain graces for us which we ourselves do not deserve. But everyone must know that, after the Mother of God, St. Joseph is, of all the saints, the one dearest to God. He has, therefore, great power with Him and can obtain graces for His devout clients. Let

us then frequently say:

**St. Joseph, give me the greatest confidence in thy powerful intercession.*

SECOND DAY

We should, indeed, honour St. Joseph, since the Son of God Himself was graciously pleased to honour him by calling him father. "Christ," says Origen, "gave to Joseph the honour due to a parent." The Holy Scriptures speak of him as the father of Jesus. "His father and mother were marvelling at the things spoken concerning Him" *(Luke 2:33)*. Mary also used this name: "in sorrow thy father and I have been seeking thee" *(Luke 2:48)*. If, then, the King of Kings was pleased to raise Joseph to so high a dignity, it is right and obligatory on our part to endeavour to honour him as much as we can.

**St. Joseph, I consecrate myself to thy service forever. Protect me all the days of my life.*

THIRD DAY

The example of Jesus Christ, Who wished to honour St. Joseph so much, and to be subject to him on earth, ought to inflame all with a fervent devotion towards this great saint. Since the Eternal Father shared His own authority with St. Joseph, Jesus always regarded him as a father, and respected and obeyed him for thirty years. St. Luke says He "was subject to them" *(Luke 2:51)*. These words mean that during all this time the sole occupation of the Redeemer was to

obey Mary and Joseph. To St. Joseph, as head of the little family, belonged the office of commanding, and to Jesus as a subject, the duty of obedience. Hence, a learned author has justly said: "Men should pay great honour to him whom the King of Kings wished to raise to such a height".

St. Joseph, by the obedience which Jesus rendered to thee, make me always obedient to the will of God.

FOURTH DAY

St. Bernardine of Siena says that we should be persuaded that Our Lord, Who respected St. Joseph on earth as His father, will refuse Him nothing in heaven; but on the contrary, will most abundantly grant His petitions. Jesus Himself advised St. Margaret of Cortona to cherish a special devotion to St. Joseph, and never to allow a day to pass without rendering some homage to him as His virginal father. Let us not, then, fail to recommend ourselves each day to St. Joseph and to ask him for graces.

St. Joseph, make me faithful in invoking you daily.

FIFTH DAY

All the faithful should be devoted to St. Joseph in order to obtain the grace of a good death, and this for three reasons. 1. Because Jesus Christ loved him not only as a friend, but as a father, and, therefore, his intercession is more powerful than that of the other saints. 2. Because Our Lord, in return for having saved Him from Herod, has given St. Joseph the special privilege of protecting the dying against the

snares of the devil. 3. Because St. Joseph, who died in the company of Jesus and Mary, is the model of a holy death and can obtain this grace for his clients.

St. Joseph, obtain for me that, like thee, I may die in the arms of Jesus and Mary.

SIXTH DAY

According to St. John Damascene: "God gave St. Joseph the love, the care, and the authority of a father over Jesus. He gave him the affection of a father that he might guard Him with great love; the solicitude of a father, that he might watch over Him with care; and the authority of a father that he might feel sure that he would be obeyed in all that he arranged concerning this Son".

St. Joseph, be always a father to us; and grant that we may be always thy faithful children.

SEVENTH DAY

When God, destines anyone for a particular office, He gives him the graces that fit him for it. Therefore, since God chose St. Joseph to fill the office of father over the person of the Incarnate Word, we must certainly believe that he conferred upon him all the sanctity which belonged to such an office. Gerson says that among other privileges Joseph had three which were special to him. First, That he was sanctified in his mother's womb, as were Jeremiah and St. John the Baptist. Second, That he was at the same time confirmed in grace. Third, That he was always exempt from the inclinations of concupiscence - a

privilege with which St. Joseph by the merit of his purity, favours his devout clients by delivering them from carnal appetites.

**St. Joseph, shining light of chastity, preserve the angelic virtue in me.*

EIGHTH DAY

In the Gospels St. Joseph is called "just". What is meant by a just man? St. Peter Chrysologus says: "It means a perfect man - one who possesses all virtues". Joseph was already holy before his marriage; but how much must his sanctity have increased after his union with the Blessed Virgin? The example of his holy spouse sufficed to sanctify him; and since Mary is the dispenser of all the graces which God grants to men, in what profusion must she not have showered them down upon her spouse, who she loved so much and by whom she was so tenderly loved!

**St. Joseph, increase my devotion to Mary.*

NINTH DAY

The two disciples, going to Emmaus were inflamed with divine love by the few moments which they spent in company with our Saviour, and by His words. What flames of holy love must not, then, have been enkindled in the heart of St. Joseph, who for thirty years conversed with Jesus Christ, and listened to His words of eternal life; who observed the perfect example which Jesus gave of humility and patience, and saw the promptness with which He obeyed and

helped him in his labours, and all that was needed for the household!

**St. Joseph, inflame us with the love of Jesus.*

TENTH DAY

St. Paul writes that in the next life Jesus Christ "will render to every man according to His works" *(Rom 2:6)*. What great glory must we not suppose that He has bestowed upon St. Joseph, who served and loved Him so much while He lived on earth! Our Lord has promised a reward to him who gives a cup of cold water to the poor in His name. What, then, must be the reward of St. Joseph, who can say to Jesus Christ: "I not only provided Thee with food, with a dwelling, and with clothes, but I saved Thee from death, delivering Thee from the hands of Herod".

**St. Joseph, increase our zeal for growing in holiness by the hope of eternal reward.*

ELEVENTH DAY

We must believe that the life of St. Joseph, spent in the presence of Jesus and Mary, was a continual prayer, abounding in acts of faith, confidence, love, resignation, and oblation. Since, then, the reward of the saints corresponds to their merits during life, consider how great must be the glory of St. Joseph in heaven. St. Augustine compares the other saints to the stars, but St. Joseph to the sun.

It is, then, very reasonable to suppose that St. Joseph,

after Mary, surpasses all the other saints in merit and glory. The Venerable Bernardine de Bustis says that when St. Joseph asks any grace for those who are devoted to him, his prayers have in a certain manner the force of a command with Jesus and Mary.

St. Joseph, obtain for us a great spirit of prayer.

TWELFTH DAY

To prove the power which St. Joseph possesses in paradise, St. Bernardine of Siena writes thus: "We cannot doubt that Christ accords to St. Joseph, now that he is in heaven, even more perfectly the respect and reverence which He paid to him on earth. Our Lord, Who on earth revered St. Joseph as His father, will certainly deny him nothing that he asks in heaven". Let us then say to him with confidence:

St. Joseph, powerful protector of souls, keep us from all sin.

THIRTEENTH DAY

O great St. Joseph, since God has served thee, I also wish to enroll myself in thy service. I wish henceforth to serve thee, to honour and love thee. Take me under thy protection and dispose of me as thou pleasest. My holy St. Joseph, pray to Jesus for me. Having obeyed all thy commands on earth, He will certainly never refuse anything thou ask of Him. Tell Him to pardon me the offences that I have committed against Him. Tell Him to detach me from creatures and from myself. Ask Him to inflame me with His holy love.

St. Joseph, watch over us, thy children.

FOURTEENTH DAY

Most holy Patriarch, now that you are on a lofty throne in heaven near thy beloved Jesus, Who was subject to thee on earth, have pity on me, who am exposed to the attacks of so many enemies, to the evil spirits, and the passions that continually strive to rob me of the grace of God. Through the grace given to thee on earth of enjoying the continual society of Jesus and Mary, obtain for me the grace of living during the remaining days of my life united to God, by resisting the attacks of hell. Grant, too, that I may die with the love of Jesus and Mary in my heart so that I may be able one day to enjoy with thee, their company in the kingdom of heaven.

**St. Joseph, grant me a horror of sin and the grace to conquer my passions.*

FIFTEENTH DAY

St. Bernard, speaking of St. Joseph's power of dispensing graces to his devout servants, makes use of the following remarkable words: "To some of the saints power is granted to succour us in particular necessities; but to St. Joseph power is granted to succour in all necessities, and to defend all those who, with devotion, have recourse to him." Let us then often say to him:

**St. Joseph, help us when we are in need.*

SIXTEENTH DAY

St. Teresa says: "I do not remember to have asked any

favour from St. Joseph which he did not grant. An account of the many graces which God has bestowed upon me, and of the dangers, corporal and spiritual, from which He has delivered me through this saint would excite wonder. The Lord appears to have given power to the other saints to assist us in a single necessity; but experience shows that St. Joseph gives aid in all. The Lord gives us to understand that, as He was to be subject to St. Joseph on earth, so in heaven He does whatever the saint asks".

St. Joseph, obtain for me the grace of perseverance in prayer.

SEVENTEENTH DAY

St. Teresa also writes: "I would wish to persuade all the world to be devoted to St. Joseph, because I have long experience of the great favours which he obtains from God. I have never known any soul especially devoted to him that did not always advance in virtue. I ask, for God's sake, that they who do not believe me will at least make a trial of this devotion. I cannot believe that favours are not granted to St. Joseph in return for the help which he gave on earth to Jesus and Mary".

St. Joseph, patron of the interior life, lead me to that perfection which God requires of me.

EIGHTEENTH DAY

Let us ask St. Joseph for the grace to love our Lord Jesus Christ. This is the particular grace which St. Joseph obtains for those who are devout to him-a tender love toward the Incarnate Word. The saint merited the power to bestow this grace upon his servants by the great love which he himself bore toward Jesus while he lived on earth.

St. Joseph, make me love Jesus with all my heart.

NINETEENTH DAY

When Jesus lived in this world in the house of St. Joseph, could a sinner who desired to obtain forgiveness from Our Lord have found a more efficacious means of obtaining pardon than through St. Joseph? If, then, we desire to receive the forgiveness of our sins, let us have recourse to St. Joseph who, now that he is in heaven, is more loved by Jesus Christ than he was loved by Him on earth.

St. Joseph, obtain from Jesus the pardon of my sins.

TWENTIETH DAY

"And Joseph also went from Galilee out of the town of Nazareth into Judea to the town of David, which is called Bethlehem" *(Luke 2:4)*. In response to the decree of Caesar Augustus, St. Joseph made the long journey across the hills from Galilee to Bethlehem with Mary, who bore beneath her heart the Incarnate Son of God. What sweet conversations must Mary and Joseph have held on this journey on the mercy of God in sending His Son into the world to redeem the human race, and on the love of this Son in coming into this valley of tears in order to atone by His suffering and death for the sins of men!

St. Joseph, I wish to belong entirely to thee, so that through

thee I may belong entirely to Jesus and Mary.

TWENTY-FIRST DAY

"And it came to pass while they were there, that the days for her to be delivered were fulfilled. And she brought forth her firstborn son, and wrapped him in swaddling clothes, and laid him in a manger, because there was no room for them in the inn" *(Luke 2:6-7)*. How great must have been the sorrow of St. Joseph when he could find no shelter for Mary on the night of the birth of the Divine Word, and was obliged to bring her to a stable! How his heart must have been pierced with anguish to see his holy spouse, who was pregnant, and near the time of childbirth, trembling with cold in that damp cave, which was open on every side. Dear St. Joseph, through the pain which you felt in seeing the Divine Word born in a stable, so poor, without fire, without clothes,, and in hearing the cries caused by the cold which afflicted Him, I pray thee to obtain for me a true sorrow for my sins by which I have drawn tears from Jesus.

**St. Joseph, penetrate my heart with contrition and obtain for me the grace never to sin again.*

TWENTY-SECOND DAY

"And she brought forth her firstborn son, and wrapped him in swaddling clothes, and laid him in a manger" *(Luke 2:7)*. How great must have been the joy of St. Joseph when he heard Mary calling him and saying "Joseph, come, and adore our infant God, Who is just born in this cave. Behold how beautiful

He is. Look at the King of the world in this manger, on this straw. See how He, who makes the seraphs burn with love, trembles with cold. Behold how He who is the joy of paradise weeps"! Dear St. Joseph, through the joy which you received at the first sight of the infant Jesus in the crib, so beautiful and lovely that your heart began from that moment to beat with love for Him alone, obtain for me also the grace to love Jesus with an ardent love on earth so that I may one day go to enjoy Him in heaven.

**St. Joseph, share with me a little of the burning love that thou didst bear to Jesus.*

TWENTY-THIRD DAY

"Glory to God in the highest and on earth peace among men of good will" *(Luke 2:14)*. Consider how great was the love and tenderness of St. Joseph when he beheld with his own eyes the Son of God become an infant; when he heard the angels singing around their newborn Lord, and saw the stable filled with light. Kneeling down and weeping with love and compassion, Joseph said: "I adore Thee, yes I adore Thee, my Lord and my God. How great is my happiness to be the first, after Mary, to see Thee born, and to know that in this world Thou wishest to be called and reputed my Son! Allow me, then, also to call Thee my Son, and to say: My God and my Son, to Thee I consecrate my whole being. My life shall be no longer mine, but shall be thine without reserve"!

**St. Joseph, grant that I may spend my life, like thee, in the*

service of God.

TWENTY-FOURTH DAY

"An angel of the Lord appeared in a dream to Joseph, saying, 'Arise, and take the child and His mother and flee into Egypt" *(Matt. 2:13)*. Consider the ready obedience of St. Joseph, who raised no doubts about the time of the journey, nor about the manner of travelling, nor about the place in Egypt in which they were to stay, but immediately prepared to set out. He instantly makes known to Mary the command of the angel, and on the same night sets out without guide on a journey of 400 miles through mountains, across rugged roads and deserts.

**My holy protector, obtain for me the grace of perfect obedience to the divine will.*

TWENTY-FIFTH DAY

How much St. Joseph must have suffered on the journey into Egypt in seeing the sufferings of Jesus and Mary! Their food must have been a piece of hard bread. They could have slept only in some poor hut, or in the open air. Joseph was indeed conformed in all things to the will of the Eternal Father, but his tender and loving heart could not but feel pain in seeing the Son of God trembling and weeping from cold and the other hardships which He experienced.

**St. Joseph, obtain for me the grace that in my journey to eternity I may never lose the company of Jesus and Mary.*

TWENTY-SIXTH DAY

"The boy Jesus remained in Jerusalem, and his parents did not know it" *(Luke 2:43)*. How great was the pain of St. Joseph when Jesus was lost in the temple! Joseph was accustomed to the enjoyment of the sweet presence of his beloved Saviour. What, then, must have been his sorrow when he was deprived of it for three days, without knowing whether he should evermore find Jesus, and most painful of all, without knowing why he had lost Him. How great, on the other hand, was Joseph's joy when he found Jesus and realised that the absence of the Child did not arise from any neglect on his part, but from a zeal for the glory of the Father.

**St. Joseph, through the merits of the pains which thou didst suffer at losing Jesus, obtain for me tears to weep always for my sins.*

TWENTY-SEVENTH DAY

"He went down with them and came to Nazareth, and was subject to them" *(Luke 2:51)*. Reflect on the holy life which Joseph led in the company of Jesus and Mary. In that family there was no business except that which tended to the greater glory of God; there were no thoughts or desires except the thought and desire of pleasing God; there were no discourses except on the love which men owe to God, and which God has shown to men, especially in sending His only begotten Son into the world to suffer and to end His life in a sea of sorrows and insults for the salvation of mankind.

**St. Joseph, through the tears which thou didst shed in contemplating the future passion of Jesus, obtain for me a continual remembrance of the suffering of my Redeemer.*

TWENTY-EIGHTH DAY

Consider the love which St. Joseph bore to Mary, his holy spouse. She was the most beautiful of all women. She was more humble, more meek, more pure, more obedient, more inflamed with the love of God, than all the angels and than all men that have been or shall be created. Hence, she merited all his love. Add to this his realisation of the love that she bore for him, and the fact that God had chosen her as His beloved Mother.

**St. Joseph, obtain for me a great love for Mary, thy most holy spouse.*

TWENTY-NINTH DAY

Consider the love which Joseph bore for Jesus. This love was not purely human like the love of other fathers, but super-human; for he loved Jesus not only as his son but also as his God. Joseph knew from the angel that his child was the Divine Word Who had become man to save mankind. He realised, too, that he himself had been chosen from among all men to be the protector and guardian of this divine Infant. What a flame of holy love must, then, have been enkindled in the heart of Joseph by reflecting on all these things, and by the sight of his Lord obeying him

like a little boy, opening and closing the door, helping him to saw or to plane, gathering fragments of wood, or sweeping the house!

**St. Joseph, remove from my heart all that could be an obstacle to the love of God.*

THIRTIETH DAY

"Precious in the eyes of the Lord is the death of His faithful ones" *(Ps.115:6).* After having faithfully served Jesus and Mary, St. Joseph reached the end of his life in the house at Nazareth. There, surrounded by angels, assisted by Jesus Christ the King of angels, and by Mary, his spouse, who placed themselves at each side of his poor bed, filled with the peace of paradise, he departed from this miserable life. Who shall ever be able to understand the sweetness, the consolation, the blessed hope, the acts of resignation, the flames of charity which the words of eternal life coming alternately from the lips of Jesus and Mary, breathed into the soul of Joseph at the end of his life?

**St. Joseph, grant me peace and resignation to God's will at the hour of my death.*

THIRTY-FIRST DAY

Great, indeed, will be the comfort of those, who, at the hour of death shall be protected by St. Joseph. For this great saint has received from God power to command the devils and to drive them away, less they tempt his servants in their dying moments. Happy is the soul that shall be assisted by this great advocate, who, on account of having died with the assistance of Jesus and Mary, and because of having preserved the infant Jesus from the danger of death by his flight into Egypt, has received the privilege of being the patron of a good death, and of delivering his clients from the danger of eternal death.

St. Joseph, defend me from the attacks of the devils at the last moment of my life.

WEDNESDAY DEVOTIONS AND VOTIVE MASS OF ST. JOSEPH

St. Joseph's Rosary

Leader: In the name of the Father, and of the Son, and of the Holy Spirit

All: Amen.

Leader: Come Holy Spirit fill the hearts of the faithful

All: And enkindle in them the fire of your love

Leader: Send forth your spirit, and they shall be created

All: And thou shall renew the face of the earth

Let us Pray

O God, who by the light of the Holy Spirit did instruct the hearts of the faithful, grant that in the same Holy Spirit, we may be truly wise and evermore rejoice in His consolation, through Christ Our Lord. Amen.

All: Glorious St. Joseph, first man to love Mary and hold Jesus in his arms, accept these prayers we now offer to honour you and ask Almighty God's blessing upon us. We pray that all the members of our families will be spiritually and physically protected through life, and guided to fulfill wisely and with love, the vocations God has given us.

Bless our families and society; bless God's family of faith in churches throughout the world; bless all the good works we do to be faithful followers of your son, Jesus. We pray especially that God will grant us the favour we now ask, if it is His will, or one that He knows is better for us (pause, *mention your intentions*). We ask this through Christ our Lord - Amen.

The Creed: I believe in God the Father Almighty......

Our Father who art in heaven ....

Mysteries of St. Joseph Rosary

1. The Virginal and Holy union of Mary and Joseph

2. The Birth of Jesus at Bethlehem

3. The Holy Name of Jesus, Our Saviour

4. The Presentation of Jesus as the First Born of the Father

5. Jesus was taken to safety in Egypt

6. Jesus Sanctifies daily life at Nazareth

7. Jesus Works alongside with Joseph

Pray the seven mysteries invoking St. Joseph's intercession with the following:

Pray on small beads:

V/. Hail, O Joseph, just man, God chose you as the spouse of Mary and Jesus honoured you with the title of father.

R/. O Guardian of the Redeemer and Patron of the Universal Church, protect our families and assist us at the hour of our death. Amen. **(7X)**

Glory be to the Father ....

Jesus have mercy of us, Mary and Joseph help us.

Hail Holy Queen, Mother of Mercy....

Litany of St. Joseph   **See page 16**

Concluding Prayer (Pope Leo XIII's Prayer to St. Joseph)

Leader: Let us Pray:

All: To you, O Blessed Joseph, we come in our trials, and having asked the help of your most holy spouse, we confidently ask your patronage also. Through that sacred bond of charity which united you to the Immaculate Virgin Mother of God and through the fatherly love with which you embraced the Child Jesus, we humbly beg you to look graciously upon the beloved inheritance which Jesus Christ purchased by his blood, and to aid us in our necessities with your power and strength. O most provident guardian of the Holy Family, defend the chosen children of Jesus Christ. Most beloved father, dispel the evil of falsehood and sin. Our most mighty protector, graciously assist us from heaven in our struggle with the powers of darkness. And just as you once saved the Child Jesus from mortal danger, so now defend God's Holy Church from the snares of

her enemies and from all adversity. Shield each one of us by your constant protection, so that, supported by your example and your help, we may be able to live a virtuous life, to die a holy death, and to obtain eternal happiness in heaven. Amen.

Seven Sorrows & Joys of St. Joseph

(This could serve for the seven Sunday devotions before March 19, if prayed with the readings and reflecting on the passages provided.)

All: Glorious St. Joseph, first man to love Mary and hold Jesus in his arms, accept these prayers we now offer to honour you and ask Almighty God's blessing upon us. We pray that all the members of our families will be spiritually and physically protected through life, and guided to fulfill wisely and with love, the vocations God has given us. Bless our families and society; bless God's family of faith in churches throughout the world; bless all the good works we do to be faithful followers of your son, Jesus. We pray especially that God will grant us the favour we now ask, or if it is His will, or one that He knows is better for us (pause, *mention your intentions*). We ask this through Christ our Lord - Amen.

1st **Sorrow** – Joseph's quandary at Mary's Pregnancy
(Matthew 1:18-19)
1st **Joy** – The Annunciation to St. Joseph *(Matthew 1:20-21)*

Leader: Chaste Lover of Mary, how overwhelmed you were when you thought that you would have to end your betrothal to her. But when the angel of God came to you in a dream, you were filled with awe to realise that Mary would be your wife, and you would be the guardian of the Messiah.

All: Help us St. Joseph, help our families and all our loved ones to overcome all sadness of heart and develop an absolute trust in God's goodness.

Our Father…, Hail Mary…, Glory Be….

2ⁿᵈ Sorrow – The Poverty of Jesus' Birth *(Luke 2:6-7)*
2ⁿᵈ Joy – The Birth of the Savior of Mankind *(Luke 2:10-19)*

Leader: Faithful guardian of Jesus, what a failure you thought you were when you could only provide a stable for the birth of the Holy Child. And then what a wonder it was when shepherds came to tell of angel choirs, and wise men came to adore the King of Kings.

All: Through your example and prayers, help us St. Joseph and all we love to become like sinless mangers where the Saviour of the world may be received with absolute love and respect.

Our Father…, Hail Mary…, Glory Be….

3rd Sorrow – The pain of the Circumcision of Jesus *(Luke 2:21)*
3rd Joy – The Holy Name of Jesus *(Matthew 1:24-25)*

Leader: Tender-hearted Joseph, you too felt pain when the blood of Jesus was first shed at His circumcision. Yet how proud you were to be the one privileged to give the name Jesus to the very Son of God.

All: Pray for us St. Joseph, that the sacred blood of Christ, poured out for our salvation, may guard our families, so the Divine Name of Jesus may be written in our hearts forever.

Our Father…, Hail Mary…, Glory Be….

4th Sorrow – Simeon's Prophecy of the Sword of sorrows *(Luke 2:34-35)*
4th Joy – The Salvation of Mankind *(Luke 2:29-33)*

Leader: Joseph, loving husband, how bewildered you were when Simeon spoke the words of warning that the hearts of Jesus and Mary would be pierced with sorrows. Yet his prediction that this would lead to the salvation of innumerable souls filled you with consolation.

All: Help us, St. Joseph, to see with the eyes of faith that even the sorrows and pains of those we deeply love can become the pathway to salvation and eternal life.

Our Father…, Hail Mary…, Glory Be….

5th Sorrow – The Flight into Egypt *(Matthew 2:13-14)*
5th Joy – The Toppling of the Idols *(Isaiah 19:1)*

Leader: Courageous protector of the Holy Family, how terrified you were when you had to make the sudden flight with Jesus and Mary to escape the treachery of King Herod and the cruelty of his soldiers. But when you reached Egypt, what satisfaction you had to know that the Saviour of the world had come to replace the pagan idols.

All: Teach us by your example, St. Joseph, to keep far away from the false idols of earthly attractions, so that like you, we may be entirely devoted to the service of Jesus and Mary.

Our Father…, Hail Mary…, Glory Be….

6th Sorrow – The Perilous Return from Exile *(Matthew 2:19-22)*
6th Joy – Family Life at Nazareth *(Luke 2:39-40)*

Leader: Ever-obedient Joseph, you trustingly returned to Nazareth at God's command, in spite of your fear that King Herod's son might still be a threat to Jesus' life. Then what fatherly pride you had in seeing Jesus grow in wisdom and grace before God and men under your care.

All: Show us St. Joseph, how to be free from all useless fear and worry, so we may enjoy the peace of a tranquil conscience, living safely with Jesus and Mary in our hearts.

Our Father…, Hail Mary…, Glory Be….

7ᵗʰ Sorrows – The Loss of the Child Jesus *(Luke 2:45)*
7ᵗʰ Joy – The Finding of the Child Jesus *(Luke 2:46)*

Leader: Dependable father and husband, how anguished you and Mary were when you searched for three days to find Jesus, lost through no fault of your own. What incredible relief was yours when you found Him safe in the Temple of God.

All: Help us St. Joseph, never to lose Jesus through the fault of our own sins. But if we should lose Him, lead us back with unwearied sorrow, until we find Him again; so that we, like you, may finally pass from this life, dying safely in the arms of Jesus and Mary.

Our Father…, Hail Mary…, Glory Be….

Leader: Pray for us, holy Joseph.

All: That we may be made worthy of the promises of Christ.

Let us Pray
O blessed St. Joseph, tender-hearted father, faithful guardian of Jesus, chaste spouse of the Mother of God, I pray and beseech you to offer to God the

Father my praise to Him through his divine Son, who died on the cross and rose again to give us sinners new life. Through the holy name of Jesus, pray with us that we may obtain from the eternal Father, the favour we ask *(pause, mention your intentions)*. We have been unfaithful to the unfailing love of God the Father; beg of Jesus mercy for us. Amid the splendours of God's loving presence, do not forget the sorrows of those who suffer, those who pray, those who weep. By your prayers and those of your most holy spouse, our Blessed Lady, may the love of Jesus answer our call of confident hope. Amen.

Prayer to St. Joseph for Workers

All: O glorious St. Joseph, under the humble appearance of a workman, you have hidden your unique and royal dignities of guardian of Jesus and Mary, and by your toil have supported them. Protect in your love and power the workers who are specially entrusted to you. You know their anxieties and sufferings, because you have undergone them yourself with Jesus and Mary at your side. Do not allow that laden with the cares of the world, they forget the end for which they have been created by God; do not let mistrust get hold of their immortal souls. Remind all workers in fields, schools, offices, factories, mines, markets and laboratories that they are not isolated in their work, in their joys and in their trials, but that Jesus and Mary, His mother and ours, are standing beside them to support them, to wipe their sweat and bless their fatigue. Teach them to change labour into a means of high sanctification as you did. Amen.

Prayer to St. Joseph for the Unemployed
All: O St. Joseph, we pray to you for those who are out of work, for those who want to earn their living and support their families. You who are the patron of workers; grant that unemployment may vanish from our ranks, that all those who are ready to work may put their strength and abilities into serving their fellow men and earn a just salary.

You are the patron of families; do not let those who have children to support and raise, lack the necessary means. Have pity on our brothers and sisters held down in unemployment and poverty because of sickness or social disorders. Help our political leaders and captains of industry find new and just solutions: may each and every one have the joy of contributing, according to his abilities, to the common prosperity. Grant that we may all share together in the abundant good God has given and that we may help the under privileged ones. Amen.

Leader: Glory be to the Father...............

All: As it was in the beginning..........

Jesus, Mary and Joseph, Make our families like yours.

<u>Votive Mass in Honour of St. Joseph</u>

According to the decree from the Apostolic Penitentiary, Wednesday is "a day dedicated to the memory of the Saint according to the Latin tradition." When not impeded by an obligatory memorial, feast or privileged season, Priests are encouraged to celebrate a Votive Mass of St. Joseph *(Roman Missal, Votive Masses, n. 13)* on Wednesdays while using the daily readings or choosing appropriate readings according to the General Instruction of the Roman Lectionary. These Wednesday celebrations are an opportune time to develop a catechesis on the saintly figure of St. Joseph and expound upon the virtues of Christian living and family life.

Entrance Antiphon

Behold a faithful and prudent steward, whom the Lord set over his household.

COLLECT

O God, who in your inexpressible providence were pleased to choose Saint Joseph as spouse of the most holy Mother of your Son, grant, we pray, that we, who revere him as our protector on earth, may be worthy of his heavenly intercession, through our Lord Jesus Christ, your Son, who lives and reigns with you in the unity of the Holy Spirit, God, forever and ever.

Readings: As of the Mass of the day or as permitted by the General Instruction for other Masses of St. Joseph.

As we prepare to offer the sacrifice of praise, O Holy Father, we humbly ask to be sustained in our service by the prayers of Saint Joseph, whom you called to watch like a father on earth over your Only Begotten Son. Who lives and reigns forever and ever.

Preface: The mission of Saint Joseph.

V. The Lord be with you.

R. And with your spirit.

V. Lift up your hearts.

R. We lift them up to the Lord.

V. Let us give thanks to the Lord our God.

R. It is right and just.

It is truly right and just, our duty and our salvation, always and everywhere to give you thanks, Lord, holy Father, almighty and eternal God, and in honouring Saint Joseph to give you fitting praise, to glorify you and bless you. For this just man was given by You as spouse to the Virgin Mother of God and as a wise and faithful Servant in charge of your household to watch like a father over your Only Begotten Son, our Lord Jesus Christ, who was Conceived by the overshadowing of the Holy Spirit. Through him the Angels praise your Majesty, Dominions adore and Powers tremble before you. Heaven and the Virtues of heaven and the blessed Seraphim worship together

with exultation. May our Voices, we pray, join with theirs in humble praise as we acclaim:

Holy, Holy, Holy Lord God of host...

COMMUNION ANTIPHON
Well done, good and faithful servant; Come, share your master's joy.

PRAYER AFTER COMMUNION
Restored by these life-giving Sacraments, Lord, may we live for you always in justice and holiness, helped by the example and intercession of Saint Joseph, who in carrying out your great mysteries served you as a man just and obedient, through Christ our Lord.

HOLY SPOUSES DEVOTION AND MASS
(As prepared and encouraged by
Fr. Larry Toschi, OSJ)

The Holy Spouses Rosary

What is the Holy Spouses Rosary?

The Holy Spouses Rosary is based upon the venerable, time-tried, and officially approved devotion known as the Marian Rosary. It complements and extends this devotion in a way that includes Saint Joseph. It is prayed using the same beads, but the "Hail Mary" is substituted by a prayer patterned after it in a way that includes Joseph and is thus directed to the "Holy Spouses" together, rather than to Mary alone. It opens with the two titles with which the angel addresses Mary and Joseph at their respective annunciations: "Mary, full of grace, and Joseph, son of David" *(Lk 1:28, Mt 1:20)*. Next, the Church's time-honored title for Mary, "Mother of God," is complemented by the Church's more recent choice of title for Joseph, "guardian of the Redeemer."[1] While Mary and Joseph are honoured, the child Jesus is eternally praised: he is the center of their family, and his name remains at the very center of this prayer, as it should for every prayer. Mary and

---

[1] *RC.*

Joseph are invoked together as "Holy Spouses" and their prayers are sought not simply for ourselves as individuals, but also for our families and communities. The prayer is:

Mary, full of grace, and Joseph, son of David; honour to you, Mother of God, and to you, guardian of the Redeemer. Eternal praise to the child with whom you formed a family, Jesus.
Holy Spouses, pray for us sinners, our families and communities, now and at the hour of our death. Amen.

Bringing together the two annunciations to Mary and Joseph and their common role of parenting and raising Jesus, the words of this prayer provide a background for the events of the coming of the Messiah into the world and for his years of hidden preparation for his public ministry. Jesus is clearly the object of these annunciations and of this attentive upbringing. The prayer puts us into living communion with Jesus through the love of his mother and earthly father.[2] Both Mary and Joseph possess the only lens through which to view firsthand the mysteries of the Incarnation and hidden life of the Son of God.

----

[2] *RVM, 2, 18.*

The Opening

Like the Marian rosary, this rosary begins with the Sign of the Cross, followed by the Apostles' Creed prayed while touching the crucifix. A fundamental article of faith expressed in the Creed is that God's only Son "was conceived of the Holy Spirit, [and] born of the Virgin Mary." This central mystery, shared by the Holy Spouses, is key to all that is contemplated in the mysteries of the Holy Spouses Rosary. On the beads adjacent to the crucifix, a preparatory "Our Father" may follow and then three "Hail Mary" for faith, hope and charity and a "Glory be." These initial prayers center us on our Catholic faith in the Trinity, the Incarnation, the infused theological virtues, and Mary's motherhood over the Church. This readies us for the individual steps accompanying each mystery. Then the Our Father…, Mary, full of grace and Joseph… (10 x), Glory be … follows each mystery announced.

1. The Betrothal *(Mt 1:18a, Lk 1:26-27, 2:4-5a).* Before the Incarnation the Immaculate Virgin and the just man are wedded to each other in true married love. The mystery of the Saviour's coming into the world begins with a betrothed couple whose relationship is based upon a desire to give themselves entirely to God's love. In ways they could not know, this betrothal "was part of the very plan of God."[3]

---

[3] *RC, 18.*

2. The Annunciation to Mary *(Lk 1:28-38)*. God chooses the Virgin Mary, betrothed to Joseph of the house of David, for the miracle of his coming in human flesh. The Son of God becomes dependant on acceptance by a human mother, and thereupon takes the nature of a tiny being in her womb.

3. The Annunciation to Joseph *(Mt 1:18b-25)*. God's design is for Mary's husband, the just man of the house of David, to continue with their plans to form a home together, and to name and act as father to the child conceived by the Holy Spirit. The Son of God depends upon a chosen human father, committed in a virginal marriage, to provide a loving, caring, and wholesome home for him.

4. The Visitation *(Lk 1:39-48)*. The Virgin Mary who has conceived by the Holy Spirit encounters her cousin Elizabeth who has miraculously conceived a child in her old age. John the Baptist leaps for joy in Elizabeth's womb at the encounter with Jesus in Mary's. Filled with the Holy Spirit, Elizabeth recognizes the tiny unborn Jesus as her Lord.

5. The Birth of Jesus *(Lk 2:6-16)*. The Son of God is born in the poverty of a stable in the town of David, received by the love of the humble Holy Spouses, and adored by poor shepherds.

6. The Circumcision and Naming of Jesus *(Lk 2:21)*. The covenant of Abraham and the law are brought to

fulfillment with the circumcision of the Son of God on the eighth day. The Holy Spouses give him the name they received from the angel, JESUS, indicating that the fullness of salvation has arrived.

7. The Presentation of Jesus *(Lk 2:22-35)*. As the Holy Spouses fulfill all the prescriptions of the Law of the Lord in offering the pure child in the temple, they rejoice at Simeon's prophecy of light for the nations and they grieve at the thought of the sword of rejection.

8. The Flight to and Return from Egypt *(Mt 2:13-15)*. The newborn King depends on Joseph to protect him from the bloody earthly king. Returning from Egypt, the Son of God establishes the New Covenant, leading us from the slavery of sin into the new promised land, his kingdom.

9. The Finding of Jesus in the Temple *(Lk 2:41-50)*. At the age of twelve Jesus stays behind in the temple, amazing the teachers by his understanding. His parents, Joseph and Mary, first are anguished at his being lost and then are confronted with the mystery of Jesus' reference to the temple as His "Father's house."

10. The Hidden Life at Nazareth *(Lk 2:51-52; 3:23)*. The Incarnate Son of God for thirty years lives obedient to his parents in an ordinary, hidden life of prayer, family, and work, before beginning his public

ministry. Mary and Joseph secretly ponder and guard the mystery of God sanctifying our everyday lives[4] and calling us to holiness in the ordinary.

Holy Spouses Litany

Lord, have mercy	Lord, have mercy
Christ, have mercy	Christ, have mercy
Lord, have mercy	Lord, have mercy
God our Father in heaven	have mercy on us
God the Son, Redeemer of the world	have mercy on us
God the Holy Spirit	have mercy on us
Holy Trinity, one God	have mercy on us
Holy Mary	pray for us
Saint Joseph	pray for us
Holy Spouses	pray for us
Holy parents of Jesus	pray for us
Holy protectors of the Body of Christ	pray for us
Teachers of the Holy Child	pray for us
Holy Virgins	pray for us
Spouses most loving	pray for us
Spouses most faithful	pray for us
Spouses most pure	pray for us
Spouses most just	pray for us
Spouses most obedient	pray for us
Spouses most humble	pray for us
Spouses most generous	pray for us
Models of family life	pray for us
Models for couples	pray for us

---

[4] *YOUCAT, Youth Catechism of the Catholic Church*, 2011, 86.

Models of parenthood	pray for us
Parents to those without parents	pray for us
Patrons of the unborn	pray for us
Models for virgins	pray for us
Lovers of poverty	pray for us
Comfort of the troubled	pray for us
Patrons of emigrants	pray for us
Servants of the Lord	pray for us
Ministers of Salvation	pray for us
Mother and Patron of the Church	pray for us

Lamb of God, who takes away the sins of the world, spare us, O Lord

Lamb of God, who takes away the sins of the world, hear us, O Lord

Lamb of God, who takes away the sins of the world, have mercy on us

V. The Virgin Mary was betrothed to Joseph of the House of David

R. Jesus was obedient to them and grew in wisdom, stature and grace.

Let us Pray:

Holy Father, who joined together by a virginal bond the glorious Mother of your Son and the just man, Saint Joseph, that they might be faithful cooperators in the mystery of the Word Incarnate, we beseech you, that by meditating upon the mysteries of the Incarnation and hidden life of your only begotten Son, we may live in more intimate union with Christ and walk more joyfully in the way of love, through the same Christ our Lord. Amen.

Mass of the Holy Spouses (Approved Liturgical Rite for Oblates of St. Joseph - January 23 or transferred to January 19 or 29 in USA)

Entrance Antiphon
Hail Mary, Mother of God, united by a sacred bond to Joseph, faithful guardian of your virginal motherhood.

COLLECT
Holy Father, who joined together by a virginal bond the glorious Mother of your Son and the just man, Saint Joseph, that they might be faithful cooperators in the mystery of the Word Incarnate, grant, we pray, that we who are united with you by the bond of baptism may live more intimately our union with Christ and may walk more joyfully in the way of love. Through our Lord Jesus Christ, your Son, who lives and reigns with you in the unity of the Holy Spirit, God, forever and ever.

First Reading *(Is 61:9-11)* Lectionary for the Common of the Blessed Virgin Mary [707,9]. I rejoice heartily in the Lord, for he has clothed me with a robe of salvation.

Responsorial *Psalm (Ps 113)*

R. Blessed be the name of the Lord, both now and forever.

Praise, you servants of the Lord, praise the name of the Lord.

R. Blessed be the name of the Lord, both now and forever.

From the rising to the setting of the sun is the name of the Lord to be praised.

R. Blessed be the name of the Lord, both now and forever.

 High above all nations is the Lord, above the heavens is his glory.

R. Blessed be the name of the Lord, both now and forever.

Second Reading *(Gal 4:4-7)* Lectionary for the Common of the Blessed Virgin Mary [710,3]. God sent his Son born of a woman.

Alleluia! *(Lk 2:51a)*
Jesus went down with them and came to Nazareth, and was obedient to them.

Gospel *(Lk 2:41-52)* Lectionary for the Common of the Blessed Virgin Mary: Son, why have you done this to us? Your father and I have been searching for you.

Sample Intercessions

Introduction by Celebrant

Joyously celebrating our Savior, who saw fit to be born of the Virgin Mary and to be called the son of Joseph, we present our prayers to God with confident trust.

Petitions by deacon or other minister

Let us pray together, responding:
Look on Mary and Joseph and hear our prayer. R.

Divine Master, grant that we may hear your word and keep it with pure and generous hearts, after the example of Mary, who received it and treasured it in her heart. R.

Christ, designer of the universe, known as the son of the carpenter, grant that we too may perform our daily work with generous dedication, so as to make of it an instrument of sanctification and peace. R.

Jesus, obedient son, having grown in the family of Nazareth in wisdom, age and grace before God and humanity, grant that after your example we may grow in all the virtues. R.

Jesus Redeemer, as you chose Mary and Joseph to be your guardians, so guard our families and our Congregation. R.

Celebrant's Concluding Prayer

Father of Mercy, we pray that you look with love on your family joined in prayer, so that, by imitating the humility and simplicity of the Holy Spouses, Joseph and Mary, we may obtain from you every true good, through Christ our Lord.

PRAYER OVER THE OFFERINGS

Lord, look graciously upon the gifts which we present at your altar on the Feast of the Holy Spouses, Mary and Joseph, and enkindle in us the spirit of your love, through Christ our Lord.

Preface of the Holy Spouses Mary and Joseph

V. The Lord be with you.

R. And with your spirit.

V. Lift up your hearts.

R. We lift them up to the Lord.

V. Let us give thanks to the Lord our God.

R. It is right and just.

It is truly right and just, our duty and our salvation, always and everywhere to give you thanks, Lord, holy Father, almighty and eternal God, through Jesus Christ our Lord. For you give the Church the joy of celebrating the feast of the Holy Spouses, Mary and Joseph: in her, full of grace and worthy Mother of your Son, you signify the beginning of the Church, resplendently beautiful bride of Christ; you chose him, the wise and faithful servant, as Husband of the Virgin Mother of God, and made him head of your family, to guard as a father your only Son, conceived by the work of

the Holy Spirit, Jesus Christ, our Lord. For this gift of your kindness, with the angels and saints we sing with one voice the hymn of your praise: Holy, holy, holy Lord …

Communion Antiphon *(Mt 1:20b)*

Joseph, son of David, have no fear about taking Mary as your wife, since by the Holy Spirit she has conceived this child.

PRAYER AFTER COMMUNION

Lord, by your holy gifts you have filled us with joy: by venerating the Blessed Virgin Mary and Saint Joseph, her spouse, may we be strengthened in your love and live in continual thanksgiving, through Christ our Lord.

SOLEMN BLESSINGS

Through the intercession of the Blessed Virgin Mary and of Saint Joseph, her Husband, may the Lord bless and protect you. **R.**

May his face shine upon you and may he grant you his mercy. **R.**

May he look upon you with kindness and give you his peace. **R.**

And may the blessing of almighty God, the Father, and the Son, + and the Holy Spirit, come down on you and remain with you forever. **R.**

ANNUAL DEVOTIONS, TRIDUUMS AND NOVENAS TO ST. JOSEPH

<u>Supplication to St. Joseph</u> (To be recited every year on March 19th and May 1st) translated from Italian.

In the name of the Father, and of the Son, and of the Holy Spirit. Amen!

O lovable and glorious St. Joseph, sweet guardian of the Son of God and virginal spouse of the Immaculate Conception, flower of virgins and delight of the Angels, on this day particularly solemn to you we join the Holy Virgin to thank the Lord for the immense treasures granted to your privileged soul: "You are not only a Patriarch, but prince of Patriarchs; more than a confessor; you embody the dignity of bishops, the generosity of the martyrs and the virtues of all the other Saints. More perfect than the Angels in virginity, most eminent in wisdom, most accomplished in every sort of perfection ". O dear saint, among the great, the greatest, let our hearts express to you all the most beautiful praises and all the holiest aspirations. To give you a sign of our tender affection, today we offer you our heart, so that you place it in the hands of your Jesus to purify it, to make it more disposed to the divine will, to consecrate it to the service of the Church.

Our Father, Hail Mary, Glory be to the Father.

O august protector of our families, you who have discovered the precious treasure of silence, of recollection, of interior life, bring back to our homes the value of the spiritual, the concern for the divine and the eternal, the sincere and generous search for holiness. Help us to look to heaven, to fix our poor eyes upwards, towards the blue and the peaceful. Thus purer our life will blossom and joy will shine radiantly from the faces of our children.

You who are the great patron of workers, let those who work hard here below in the workshops, factories, construction sites, fields, schools, know how to transform daily sweat into a divine gift. Bring back to the poor hearts of those who no longer think of your beloved Lord, the consoling virtues of faith, hope and charity.

Our Father, Hail Mary, Glory be to the Father

A merciful gaze, turn particularly today, to the Pope, to Bishops, to Priests, to Religious, to all Christians, O most strong Protector of the Universal Church. You, who saved Jesus from the snares of Herod, save us from sin that alone can ruin us forever; save us from the false attractions of Satan that perverts mercilessly, especially when the temptation is particularly malignant. At that moment, come to our help with your powerful intercession, so that we too can say together with your great devotee: "I don't remember asking a favour from Saint Joseph without being heard".

These are the graces we ask of you: to be able to always keep Jesus in our hearts; to love him with all our soul, with all our strength, throughout our life. That those who do not yet know the Church, who are far away, who have gone away, may return to the fold, behind your sweet call! And to whom, if not you, O sweet Patron of the dying, will we offer the last moments of our life? In that moment, on which all eternity depends, give a look as you know how to do to that Child whom you so dearly held in your arms; and with the Virgin Mary, your Bride, come to us, O powerful and merciful St. Joseph.

Our Father, Hail Mary, Glory be to the Father

<u>Triduum in Honour of St. Joseph</u> (To ask for graces) translated from Italian

To be recited in its entirety for three days in a row starting from March 16 or April 28 or whenever you want to express your devotion to the saint or ask for some special graces.

O God come to my aid. O Lord, make haste to help us.

Glory be to the Father....

Saint Joseph, my protector, I have recourse to you so that I may obtain this grace from the Sacred Heart of Jesus (*pause, mention your request*). For my sins, I do not deserve for it to be granted. Make up for my shortcomings and, mighty as you are, grant that, having obtained the desired grace through your pious intercession, I may come to your feet, to pay you the due homage of my gratitude.

Glory be to the Father ….

Do not forget, dear Saint Joseph, that no person in the world, no matter how great a sinner he was, who has turned to you, has remained disappointed in the trust and hope placed in you. Thousand of graces shine and favors abound that you have obtained by your intercession for the afflicted poor. Do not allow, oh great Saint, that I be the only one to be deprived of the grace that I ask of you. Show yourself powerful and generous also towards me, and my tongue, my soul, my heart, thanking you will sing: "Long live the glorious Patriarch St. Joseph".

Glory to the Father ….

O exalted head of the Holy Family, I venerate you deeply and, with all my heart, I invoke you. To all the afflicted souls, who have prayed to you, you have granted comfort and peace, thanks and favours. Deign, therefore, to console with your help, even my grieving soul, which finds no rest in the anguish, by which it is oppressed. You, oh great saint, see in God all my needs; therefore, you know how much the grace that I ask of you is necessary for me. If you obtain this grace for me, I promise to always love you and serve you faithfully until death. O Saint Joseph, comforter of the afflicted, show pity to my pain.

Glory be to the Father ….

Remember, virginal spouse of the Virgin Mary, o my sweet protector, Saint Joseph, that no one has ever invoked your protection and asked for your help without being consoled. With this trust, I turn to you and fervently commend myself. O father of the Redeemer, hear my prayer and favourably grant my petition. Amen.

Triduum of Thanksgiving to St. Joseph

(for graces received) translated from Italian.

The triduum of thanksgiving to St. Joseph is to be recited in its entirety for three consecutive days. It is customary to recite the triduum at the end of the month dedicated to him, from the 28th to 30th of March, or whenever you want to say thanks to Saint Joseph or express your devotion to the saint or ask for special graces.

O most holy husband of Mary, with a heart full of gratitude I come to you to thank you for having, with paternal goodness, accepted and answered my prayer. O dear Saint Joseph, as you listened to my invocation for help, now welcome my song of gratitude. No one has ever been disappointed by turning to You.

Glory be to the Father …. (3x)

Great guardian of the Incarnate Word, blessed be the moment when I confidently turned to You. My groan was heard by you, my prayer was answered by you. Be eternally blessed, o august head of the Holy Family.

Glory be to the Father …. (3x)

O exalted wonder worker, as a sign of gratitude for having experienced your power over the Hearts of Jesus and Mary, I propose to make known to everyone your dignity and power, by words and by actions, to induce everyone to turn to you, with confidence in all physical and spiritual needs.

Glory be to the Father …. (3x)

Triduum in Honour of St. Joseph the Worker

(Prayer of Saint Pius X, For the Sanctification of Labour). To be prayed from 28ᵗʰ – 30ᵗʰ April

Glorious St. Joseph, model of all workers, obtain for me the grace to work in the spirit of thanksgiving and joy. Let me consider it an honour to use and develop the gifts received from God. Aid me to work conscientiously in order, peace, and moderation, preferring my duty to my inclinations; to work in the spirit of penance for the expiation of my sins. Help me to work above all for the glory of God and not for any selfish reasons, and to keep before my eyes the account I must give of time lost and work badly done. Watch over me and give me the strength to imitate you in order that I may obtain the reward of those who work for God. Amen.

V: Glory be to the Father, and to the Son, and to the Holy Spirit:

R: as it was in the beginning, is now, and ever shall be, world without end. Amen.

V: St. Joseph our protector,

R: pray for us.

Prayer for Workers

O glorious Saint Joseph, who, under the humble appearance of a workman, have hidden your unique and royal dignity of guardian of Jesus and Mary, and by your toil have supported them, protect in your love and power the workers who are specially entrusted to you. You know their anxieties and sufferings, because you have undergone them yourself, with Jesus and Mary at your side. Do not permit that, laden with the cares of the world, they forget the end for which they have been created by God; do not let the seeds of mistrust get hold of their immortal souls. Recall to all workers in fields, schools, offices, factories, mines, markets and laboratories that they are not isolated in their work, in their joys and in their trials, but that Jesus and Mary, his mother and ours, are standing beside them to support them, to wipe their sweat and bless their fatigue. Teach them to change labour into a means of high sanctification as you did. Amen.

V: Glory be to the Father, and to the Son, and to the Holy Spirit:

R: as it was in the beginning, is now, and ever shall be, world without end. Amen.

V: St. Joseph our protector,

R: pray for us.

Novena to St. Joseph

(10th - 18th March or 22nd - 30th April, can also be prayed at other times provided it is said completely and faithfully) From Grazie San Guiseppe's web site. Translated from Italian

In the name of the Father ….

Sequence to the Holy Spirit

Come, Holy Spirit, come!
And from your celestial home
Shed a ray of light divine!

Come, Father of the poor!
Come, source of all our store!
Come, within our bosoms shine.

You, of comforters the best;
You, the soul's most welcome guest;
Sweet refreshment here below;

In our labour, rest most sweet;
Grateful coolness in the heat;
Solace in the midst of woe.

O most blessed Light divine,
May that light within us shine
And our inmost being fill!

Where you are not, we have naught,
Nothing good in deed or thought,
Nothing free from taint and ill.

Heal our wounds, our strength renew;
On our dryness pour your dew;
Wash the stains of guilt away:

Bend the stubborn heart and will;
Melt the frozen, warm the chill;
Guide the steps that go astray.

On the faithful, who adore
And confess you, evermore
In your sevenfold gift descend;

Give them virtue's sure reward;
Give them your salvation, Lord;
Give them joys that never end. Amen.

Let us pray:

O Father, who by the light of the Holy Spirit guide believers to the full knowledge of the truth, grant us to taste true wisdom in your Spirit and to always enjoy his comfort, through our Lord Jesus Christ, your Son who lives and reigns with you, in the unity of the Holy Spirit, God forever and ever. Amen.

I believe in one God, the Father Almighty....
1) Prayer of the day
2) Our Father, Hail Mary, Glory be to the Father ....
3) Supplication in honour of Joseph's hidden life with Jesus and Mary

Supplications in honour of St. Joseph's hidden life with Jesus and Mary

St. Joseph, pray that Jesus may come into my soul and sanctify me.

St. Joseph, pray that Jesus may come into my heart and inspire it with charity.

St. Joseph, pray that Jesus may come into my mind and enlighten it.

St. Joseph, pray that Jesus may guide my will and strengthen it.

St. Joseph, pray that Jesus may direct my thoughts and purify them.

St. Joseph, pray that Jesus may guide my desires and direct them.

St. Joseph, pray that Jesus may look upon my deeds and extend His blessings.

St. Joseph, pray that Jesus may inflame me with love for Him.

St. Joseph, request for me from Jesus the imitation of thy virtues.

St. Joseph, request for me from Jesus true humility of spirit.

St. Joseph, request for me from Jesus meekness of heart.

St. Joseph, request for me from Jesus peace of soul.

St. Joseph, request for me from Jesus a holy fear of the Lord.

St. Joseph, request for me from Jesus a desire for perfection.

St. Joseph, request for me from Jesus a gentleness of heart.

St. Joseph, request for me from Jesus a pure and charitable heart.

St. Joseph, request for me from Jesus the wisdom of faith.

St. Joseph, request for me from Jesus His blessing of perseverance in my good deeds.

St. Joseph, request for me from Jesus the strength to carry my crosses.

St. Joseph, request for me from Jesus a disdain for the material goods of this world.

St. Joseph, request for me from Jesus the grace to always walk on the narrow path toward Heaven.

St. Joseph, request for me from Jesus the grace to avoid all occasion of sin.

St. Joseph, request for me from Jesus a holy desire for eternal bliss.

St. Joseph, request for me from Jesus the grace of final perseverance.

St. Joseph, do not abandon me.

St. Joseph, pray that my heart may never cease to love thee and that my lips may ever praise thee.

St. Joseph, for the love thou didst bear for Jesus, grant that I may learn to love Him.

St. Joseph, graciously accept me as thy devoted servant.

St. Joseph, I give myself to thee; accept my pleas and hear my prayers.

St. Joseph, do not abandon me at the hour of my death.

Jesus, Mary and Joseph, I give Thee my heart and my soul.

Glory be to the Father (3X)

Daily Prayers:

1st day - Saint Joseph Model of Faith – March 10
Saint Joseph, on this day we look to you as a model of faith. You welcomed the presence of God into your life. On his word you committed yourself to the most impenetrable mystery, that of the incarnation of the Son of God. Your Virgin Bride conceived without human intervention: a child was born who is God; you loved and protected Him. All of this is shocking and, without faith, it would have been an impossible mystery.

But you knew that when God speaks to man, He does not deceive him. That is why, without arguing, without asking questions, you went on, happy to walk in the light, because God was there.

It is in this direction that you committed your life to that of Mary, thus obeying her will, at the same time

opening the way to the realisation of the salvation of men.

Now we too want to adhere to this faith that was yours, so that God may dwell in us and so that we may be faithful to his will. Sometimes we falter in our Christian life. We believe in God, in Christ, in the Church, but we often live on the margins of our faith. Faith has guided your whole life; let it become for us the light that continually attracts us, the guide to our daily actions. Through faith, we always feel God's hand in the events of our life, so that we can thus participate in his work of justice, peace and love. Amen.

2nd day - Saint Joseph Model of Hope – March 11

During your life, Saint Joseph, you were the man of hope. Everyone around you shared the hope of seeing their redemption accomplished one day. And behold, the Messiah, the Son of God, lives next to you, in your house, united to you as the son to the Father. It is a sign of the goodness and fidelity of the Lord. And this fidelity on the part of the Almighty in keeping His Word opened for you a prospect of limitless hope.

You, O Saint Joseph, hoped for salvation for Mary and for you, since you welcomed God himself into your life. Your only strength, in the unpredictable events that occurred to you (the painful circumstances of Jesus' birth, the flight into Egypt,

the stay in exile), was the unshakable hope in the goodness, in the power, in the faithfulness of the Lord. This is undoubtedly what explains the quiet serenity that radiates in your home.

Saint Joseph, grant that we may learn from you to hope. You know it: life does not spare us at all. From time to time our most beautiful promises fall, our most tempting desires collapse. Those who yesterday dreamed of a fruitful and delicate life, today see themselves grappling with daily pettiness; whoever promised himself yesterday to build a strong love, sees today the difficulty of loving fully; who yesterday dreamed of the good to be achieved, the struggles to be waged for the good, today finds himself facing his limits. How many even today in this moment of economic, political and moral crisis, are discouraged and sometimes let hope fall!

Saint Joseph, teach us to hope in spite of everything: evil can never discourage those who look towards God. Beyond all weaknesses there is the Creator's fidelity: it is on Him that we wish to count. Grant that there is no other way for us to live than to hope! And this hope transforms us, giving us great certainty, the taste for combat and action. Amen.

3rd day - Saint Joseph Model of Charity – March 12
Saint Joseph, you have spent your life in an atmosphere of generous love. You loved Mary, who was to bring her Son into the world. Then, with her,

you had a special part in the most beautiful act of love in the history of the world: the coming of the Son of God among men to save them.

God who is love has lived in your house. He shared your table, the intimacy of your family, your joys, your difficulties, in every moment of your life.

Since the attention of parents is concentrated on their children because they love them, all your generosity and that of Mary naturally turned to the Son of God who became your Son. Together you have loved your neighbour. You have found in this love an active part in the mystery of salvation, a gesture of perfect love for all men of the earth.

You who have found love so well in your life, teach us to love. Make us understand that love comes from God. When we are overwhelmed by misunderstanding or hatred, help us to orient our life according to his desire. We know that the day our hearts are truly open to charity, the face of the world will be changed. And the person next to us will no longer fight, but love.

Help us to see how much the Christian life is contained entirely in love and that, apart from the love of God and neighbour, everything is unimportant. Like you, Saint Joseph, we want to love God more and more and to share the same faithful and generous love with our neighbour. Amen.

4th day - Saint Joseph Father of Jesus – March 13

Saint Joseph, the people of Nazareth called Jesus your Son. And Mary said to him one day in the temple: "Your father and I have been looking for you." You knew how much human paternity went beyond the physical union of the spouses and you have truly become the human father of the Son of God.

You were a father full of love for Mary during the months leading up to the birth. You have been a constant support for her, a warm presence, and the beloved image of a father. God chose you because he knew the importance of this tenderness for Mary, the importance of the spirit with which you knew how to speak to her, treat her, comfort her in her labours or difficulties: all these contributed to forming the human character of her Son. You stood for Mary all the support on which her tenderness rested and, without vanity on your part, O Saint Joseph, Jesus was formed in her a little in your image.

You were the father of Jesus, for the education you gave him. It is you, Saint Joseph, who taught him, when he was a child, all those things that are learned in the company of a father. You initiated Him to life. Under your influence his spirit opened, he admired with you the lilies of the fields, the birds of the sky, the vineyards, the wheat fields. With you, Saint Joseph, through the earth, the immensity of these realities penetrated him. With him, without knowing it, you then prepared the most beautiful pages of the Gospel.

Saint Joseph, teach us to love our children like you, to give them, through our love, faith, hope, devotion, respect for all that is beautiful; a vision of the world that commits them to follow your Son on the very important path of their life. Amen.

5th day - Saint Joseph Husband of the Mother of God – March 14

St. Joseph, when one knows Mary's faith, her love, her courage, her purity, one understands your happiness at having had her as a bride: she who was worthy of the Son of God. As in a truly human family, you were her husband and she was your bride. Her heart belonged to you, you loved each other as a couple, with tender love, full of attention, which reveals a truly human attachment through the smallest gestures; strong and vigorous love that solidly unites two people, for whom no difficulty, no violence, no misfortune, can breach.

Pure and free love that pulls the flesh with it, in overcoming its defects and weaknesses. The Virgin Mary had entrusted her soul and body to you, she remained a virgin because you desired it with her. And your mutual love blossomed into virginity as a sign from God for men. As Adam and Eve had rejected God in the unity of their love, so it is in your union with Mary that Christ the Saviour came among us.

Saint Joseph, teach us to love; not in a selfishness where everyone closes in on himself and hardens

against the other, but in a generous gift that engages us in the ways of tenderness, delicacy, dedication. We know well that whoever claims to love and thinks only of himself is a liar. Teach us the truth in love, so that we can recognise its presence in us. We have been entrusted to each other to save ourselves together; teach us, Saint Joseph, respect for the other.

You who opened the way to the salvation of the world in the purity of your love, enable us to welcome the Son of God as you did and to be his witnesses in today's world. Amen.

6th day - Saint Joseph Man of Prayer - March 15

At the end of your days, Saint Joseph, you found yourself in the company of Mary to take care of Jesus. The Son of God needed his humanity to be formed like that of other children. And according to Jewish tradition it was the father's task to explain the Bible, to pass on the commandments, according to the Lord's prescription: "You will repeat them to your children" *(Deut 6: 7).*

In the company of Mary, you told him all that God had done for his people; you showed him how every gesture, every custom, had a sacred meaning. The father was entrusted with the moral and religious education of the children; you would not have missed this great mission, in which your fatherhood found its fulfillment.

Mary, next to you, listened, accomplished. Together you have thus formed the human soul of your Son, making him understand the great lessons of his Heavenly Father.

Like any faithful Jew, you prayed in the morning, in the evening and during the day; recite aloud the litanies of praise that glorified the Lord, the only true God, who makes everything live on earth and from whom all wisdom and holiness come.

You have certainly recited this prayer together: "Listen, O Israel: the Lord is our God, the Lord is one. You will love the Lord your God with all your heart, with all your soul and with all your strength"*(Deut 6: 4-5)*.

You, Saint Joseph, slowly said the holy words, so that Mary could make your Son repeat them. Accustomed to the Word of God, you then had to pray freely amidst joys and sorrows, and perhaps above all when the mystery became too great before you.

Saint Joseph, teach us to pray, and grant us to love those moments when alone, with our loved ones or with the whole Christian community, we invite God to share our life. Amen.

7th day - Saint Joseph Model of the Just man – March 16

Saint Joseph, help us to be righteous. You know that in order to fully live life as man, one must first of all

adapt one's heart and spirit to that of the Creator. Your Son did not ask first of all for an edifying exterior, for pious manners, but for a soul truly conforming to the will of God. To those who were content with external prayers and rites, He said: "It is not those who say Lord, Lord, who will be saved, but those who do the Will of my Father". Welcoming God's presence every day, living with him, is the central act of all human life.

As a well-tuned instrument produces right notes, you, Saint Joseph, knew how to live in accord with God; and the gospel could tell of you that you were a righteous man.

For the one who looked at you, your life could seem trivial: the little daily life to start over every day, the same gestures repeated hundreds of times, the same tools, the same movements, the same pauses. But you were able to put so much joy and fidelity into it that, before God, you were worthy of his Son.

In a sharing of family love, you worked, lived, suffered, loved. You have fulfilled the mission received according to the paths traced by the intelligence and love of God. And in a discreet reserve, you have accomplished a unique task, happy to feel fully faithful.

Saint Joseph, teach us to be righteous. Teach us sharing, which is a form of love. Above all, teach us justice, so that we can joyfully do the will of our Father who loves us. Amen.

8th day - Saint Joseph the Good Worker – March 17

At the beginning of the world, in the plans of the Creator, work was beautiful and good. Man has distanced himself from God and now work is faced with difficulties, hardships and pains. St. Joseph, you have submitted to this harsh law of work, because you knew that it can become noble and beautiful again according to the plans of the Creator.

This has been the secret of your life as a worker.
When God wanted an adoptive father for his Son, he chose a worker, thus demonstrating his esteem for work. You have not disappointed him. You worked with your heart and your job became an expression of love, like prayer or fidelity to the Lord.

Today we can easily imagine your sweat-wet forehead, your face lit up with a smile, as you walked along the road to Nazareth, with the sack of tools on your shoulder. You were a man: a carpenter. You bent over the pieces of wood to cut, plane, saw, nail. You did all the familiar gestures and those of the trade.

And your work, similar in all respects to that of other men, stood out, however, because it was done by one who lived in the presence of God.

St. Joseph, with your work you have been able to reach

God himself. Teach us the love of our work, let it become a source of vitality and happiness for us; that we can do it with justice and honesty; that we know how to penetrate it with lively charity, and that, following your example, we know how to welcome your Son in our workshops, in our construction sites, in our offices, and in all workplaces. St. Joseph please help all people looking for a job; remove all worries from their hearts and provide the stability they seek to live in dignity and to be able to provide for the good of all their loved ones and all the people entrusted to them. Amen.

9th day - Saint Joseph Model of Obedience - March 18

Saint Joseph, one of the most visible traits of your soul is obedience to God. Your whole life is interwoven with fidelity, obedience, and trust in the Lord who loves you.

At the beginning of the Gospel, Mary, your betrothed, is found pregnant. As a just man you decide to let go of her, in secret, so as not to harm her. But God asks you to take her as a faithful bride just the same. Attentive to this first message from God, you enter with her on the mysterious path of the Incarnation.

A few months later, the Roman emperor ordered a census in his territory. Trusting in God's ways, you accept this second trial. You leave Nazareth and go to

Bethlehem, the city of David, where the Son of God was to be born.

After the visit of the Magi, the Lord turns to you again: "Get up, take the child and his mother with you, flee to Egypt and stay there until I warn you" *(Mt 2:13)*. Without wasting a moment, once again, you get up, at night, take the Child and his Mother to go to Egypt; and stay there as long as God desires it.

A few years pass before Herod's death. Then the Lord tells you again: "Get up, take the child and his mother with you and go to the land of Israel" *(Mt 2:20)*. With admirable fidelity, you, Saint Joseph, got up, took the Child and his Mother and returned to Nazareth.

These events are enough to make us understand the greatness of your obedience. You know it well, even in our life the Lord turns to us. He speaks to us through events, in the silence of prayer, through the Church. Help us to know his voice in the midst of all the noises in the world. Help us to correspond to you, so that every day we are faithful to His love and will. Amen.

Group Novena to St. Joseph

In the name of the Father, and of the Son, and of the Holy Spirit. Amen.

Leader: Come Holy Spirit fill the hearts of the faithful

All:	And enkindle in them the fire of your love
Leader:	Send forth your spirit, and they shall be created
All:	And thou shall renew the face of the earth

Let us Pray

All: O God, who by the light of the Holy Spirit did instruct the hearts of the faithful, grant that by the same Holy Spirit, we may be truly wise and evermore rejoice in His consolation, through Christ Our Lord, Amen.

Opening Hymn

Opening prayer to St. Joseph for Faith:

Blessed St. Joseph, heir of all the Patriarchs, obtain for me this beautiful and precious virtue *(pause, mention your intentions)*. Give me a lively faith which is the foundation of all holiness, that faith without which no one can be pleasing to God. Obtain for me a faith that triumphs over all the temptations of the world and conquers human respect; a faith that cannot be shaken and that seeks God alone. In imitation of you, make me live by faith and submit my mind and heart to God, so that one day I may behold in Heaven what I now firmly believe on earth, we ask this through Christ our Lord. Amen.

Daily Novena Prayer

Blessed St. Joseph, tender hearted Father, faithful guardian of Jesus, chaste Spouse of the Mother of

God, I pray and beseech you to offer to God the Father my prayer to Him through His divine Son, who died on the cross and rose again to give us sinners new life. Through the holy name of Jesus, pray with us that we may obtain from the eternal father, the favour we ask (*pause, make your request*) We have been unfaithful to the unfailing love of God the Father; beg of Jesus mercy for us. Amid the splendours of God's loving presence, do not forget the sorrows of those who suffer, those who pray, and those who weep. By your prayers and those of your most Holy Spouse, our blessed lady, may the love of Jesus answer our call of confident hope, we ask this through Christ our Lord. Amen.

DAY 1: THE ANNUNCIATION TO JOSEPH

St. Joseph's Great Trial

Joseph had no knowledge of Mary's Divine Motherhood and he was perplexed and uncertain.

He did not know what to do about his proposed marriage. Being "a just man" he did not wish to turn Mary over to the Law or expose her to reproach. He decided to put her away quietly. He was convinced of her innocence, but he had no way of proving it to himself.

1st Reading: *Matthew 1:18-21*

(Think, Thank God, and Ask)

2nd Reading: **John Paul II**, *Redemptoris Custos* (Sections

2-3) or **Pope Francis** *Patris Corde*, Introductory Part).
One or more Decades of the St. Joseph Rosary

DAY 2: JOSEPH TAKES MARY AS HIS WIFE
Message of the Angel to Joseph

The Angel said to him: "Fear not, Joseph son of David, to take to you Mary as your wife, for that which is begotten of her is of the Holy Spirit". Further, it was made known to him that the child to be born of Mary was to be named Jesus because he would save his people from their sins.

1st Reading: *Matthew 1:20-25*

(Think, Thank God, and Ask).

2nd Reading: **John Paul II**, *Redemptoris Custos* (section 20) or **Pope Francis** *Patris Corde* (n. 1).

One or more Decades of the St. Joseph Rosary

DAY 3: THE BIRTH AND NAMING OF JESUS, SON OF DAVID
The Census

Picture Saint Joseph and Mary living quietly in Nazareth expecting the birth of the Christ Child

Suddenly notice is received that a census is to be taken and everyone must return to his own city to be enrolled. This means a great hardship for Joseph and Mary who started the journey to Bethlehem despite the hardships and difficulties they knew they would experience.

Consider Saint Joseph's inability to find a place of lodging - the need of going to a cave outside of the town - then the birth of the Christ Child. It is easy to see the four points for meditation in this wonderful scene, picturing Joseph's love and devotion as he worships the Christ Child.

1st Reading: *Lk.2:1-7*

(Think, Thank God, and Ask).

2nd Reading: **John Paul II**, *Redemptoris Custos* (sections 10-11) or **Pope Francis** *Patris Corde* (n. 2).
One or more Decades of the St. Joseph Rosary

DAY 4: JOSEPH, THE SHEPHERD AND THE MAGI

Joseph and the Birth of Christ

See how the shepherds hasten to Bethlehem to see the Christ Child and to tell the message of the Angels, "Glory to God in the highest, and peace to men of good will", it is easy to imagine the happiness of these simple shepherds, their joy and their exultation, as they worship the new - born king.

Also, think of the visit of the Magi, wise Men from the East, who have come to adore the Christ child and to offer Him the precious gifts of gold, frankincense and myrrh.

1st Reading: *Luke 2:8-20 or Matt. 2:1-12*

(Think, Thank God, and Ask).

2nd Reading: **John Paul II**, *Redemptoris Custos* (section 12) or **Pope Francis** *Patris Corde* (n. 3).
One or More Decades of the St. Joseph Rosary

DAY 5: THE PRESENTATION OF JESUS, ACCORDING TO THE LAW OF THE LORD

Joseph, Mary, Simeon and Anna with the Child

Call to mind the strong Saint Joseph carrying the Christ Child to the crowded Temple, and together with Mary present the Divine Infant to the Lord. Joseph realizes that Jesus is the light of the World and that this is the initial offering of Christ in His life of sacrifice. He bears too, with great sorrow, the words of Simeon to Mary "--- and your own soul a sword shall pierce ---"

1st Reading: *Luke 2:22-40*

(Think, Thank God, and Ask).

2nd Reading: **John Paul II**, *Redemptoris Custos* (section 13) or **Pope Francis** *Patris Corde* (n. 4).

One or more Decades of the St. Joseph Rosary

DAY 6: JOSEPH'S FLIGHT TO EGYPT WITH JESUS AND MARY

Joseph and the Flight to Egypt

Reflect on the anxiety of Saint Joseph as he is told by an Angel to take Mary and the Child and flee to Egypt. Joseph obeys at once and the Holy family departs under the cover of night. The journey is long, over four hundred miles, and difficult. For almost two years the Holy Family must remain in Egypt surrounded by strangers and in great sorrow.

1st Reading: *Matthew 2:13-22*
(Think, Thank God, and Ask).

2nd Reading: **John Paul II**, *Redemptoris Custos* (section 14) or **Pope Francis** *Patris Corde* (n. 5).

One or more Decades of the St. Joseph Rosary

DAY 7: THE FINDING OF THE CHILD JESUS IN THE TEMPLE AND THE FATHERHOOD OF JOSEPH

Joseph and Loss of Christ in Jerusalem + Joseph's Life in Nazareth

The natural anxiety of Saint Joseph for the Christ Child when it is discovered that He is not with the friends of the Holy Family can hardly be described. Frantically Joseph and Mary look for Him. After three days they find Him in the temple talking to the Doctors of the Law and asking them questions. Mary and Joseph rejoice to find Jesus again, but they hear from His lips the mysterious words: "Did you not know that I must be about my Father's business"?

1st Reading: *Luke 2:41-52*

(Think, Thank God, and Ask).

2nd Reading: **John Paul II**, *Redemptoris Custos* (Section 8) or **Pope Francis** *Patris Corde* (n. 6).

One or more Decades of the St. Joseph Rosary

DAY 8: JOSEPH THE WORKER / PATRON OF THE HIDDEN AND INTERIOR LIFE

Joseph and the Dignity of Labour

Joseph, a carpenter, teaches his Son his trade of carpentry as well as the Jewish custom. Jesus came to be identified not only as a carpenter but also as the carpenter's Son (Jn.8).

1st Reading: *Matthew 13:53-55a*

(Think, Thank God, and Ask).

2nd Reading: **John Paul II**, *Redemptoris Custos* (section 22, 24, 25-27) or **Pope Francis** *Patris Corde* (n. 7).

One or more Decades of the St. Joseph Rosary

DAY 9: THE DEATH OF ST. JOSEPH: PATRON AND MODEL OF THE CHURCH

The Death of Saint Joseph

Sacred Scripture says nothing about the death of Saint Joseph and we must supply what took place as best we can. See Saint Joseph on his death bed realising the graces which God gave him during his life, fully conscious of the value of the life of grace and virtue over that of the life of the world. One can presume that Jesus and Mary were at his bed and they comforted him. Saint Joseph is the Patron of a Happy Death for this reason - that he died in the presence of Jesus and Mary.

1ˢᵗ Reading: *1 Corinthians 12:12, 27*

(Think, Thank God, and Ask).

2ⁿᵈ Reading: **John Paul II**, *Redemptoris Custos* (sections 28-30) or **Pope Francis** *Patris Corde* (Concluding Part).

One or more Decades of the St. Joseph Rosary

Examination of Conscience

Let us examine our consciences for the sins we have committed against God, against our neighbour and against ourselves. *(2 minutes silence)*

Act of Contrition

Litany to St. Joseph   **See Pg. 16**

Let us pray:

Prayer to St. Joseph (Leo XIII Prayer)

To you, O Blessed Joseph, we come in our trials, and having asked the help of your most holy spouse, we confidently ask your patronage also. Through that sacred bond of charity which united you to the Immaculate Virgin Mother of God and through the fatherly love with which you embraced the Child Jesus, we humbly beg you to look graciously upon the beloved inheritance which Jesus Christ purchased by his blood, and to aid us in our necessities with your power and strength.

O most provident guardian of the Holy Family, defend the chosen children of Jesus Christ. Most beloved father, dispel the evil of falsehood and sin. Our most mighty protector, graciously assist us from heaven in our struggle with the powers of darkness. And just as you once saved the Child Jesus from mortal danger, so now defend God's Holy Church from the snares of her enemies and from all adversity. Shield each one of us by your constant protection, so that, supported by your example and your help, we may be able to live a virtuous life, to die a holy death, and to obtain eternal happiness in heaven. Amen.

Memorare to St. Joseph

Remember, O most chaste spouse of the Virgin Mary, that never was it known that anyone who fled to your protection, implored your help, or sought your intercession was left unassisted. Full of confidence in your power, I fly unto you and beg your protection. Despise not, O Guardian of the Redeemer, my humble supplication, but in your bounty, hear and answer me. Amen

Leader: Grant blessed Joseph that ever secure under your protection.
All: We may pass our lives free from all sin. Amen.

Closing Hymn   **See page 174 - 181**

<u>Novena For Every Kind of Need</u>
(Can be prayed at any time of the Year)

Dedication

O glorious descendant of the King of Judah! Inheritor of the virtues of all the Patriarchs! just and happy Saint Joseph! listen to my prayer. Thou art my glorious protector, and shalt ever be, after Jesus and Mary, the object of my most profound veneration and tender confidence. Thou art the most hidden, though a great saint, and art peculiarly the patron of those who serve God with the greatest purity and fervor. In union with all those who have ever been most devoted to thee, for the sake of Jesus Christ, Who vouchsafed to love and obey thee as a son, please become a father to me, and to obtain for me the filial respect, confidence, and love of a child toward thee.

O powerful advocate of all Christians! whose intercession, as Saint Teresa of Avila assures us, has never been found to fail, deign to intercede for me now, and to obtain for me the particular object of this novena (*mention your intention*). Present me, O great saint, to the Adorable Trinity, with whom thou hast so glorious and so intimate a correspondence.

Obtain that I may never efface by sin the sacred image of whose likeness I was created. Beg for me that my divine Redeemer may enkindle in my heart, and in all hearts, the fire of His love, and infuse therein the virtues of His adorable infancy, His purity, simplicity, obedience, and humility.

Obtain for me likewise a lively devotion to thy virgin spouse, and protect me so powerfully in life and death that I may have the happiness of dying as thou didst, in the friendship of my Creator, and under the immediate protection of the Mother of God.

Prayer

Glorious Saint Joseph, spouse of Mary, think of us, pray for us. Amiable Cherub, guardian of the paradise of the new Adam, labour at our sanctification. Dear virginal-father of the Sacred Victim, provide for all our present necessities. O faithful depository of the most precious of all treasures, take under thy charitable conduct the affair which we recommend to you (*mention your intention*). May its outcome be for the glory of God and the benefit of our souls. Amen.

Our Father (3x)

Hail Mary (3x) Glory Be (3x)

Holy Joseph, pray for us (3x)

Novena Prayers to St. Joseph for a Faith-Filled Spouse (For Singles)

Oh St. Joseph whose protection is so great, so strong, so prompt before the Throne of God, I place in you all my interests and desires. Oh St. Joseph do assist me by your powerful intercession and obtain for me from your Divine Son, our Lord Jesus Christ, all spiritual blessings; so that having engaged here below your Heavenly power I may offer my thanksgiving and homage to the Most Loving of Fathers. Oh St.

Joseph, I never weary contemplating you and Jesus asleep in your arms. I dare not approach while He reposes near your heart. Hold Him closer in my name and kiss His fine head for me, and ask Him to return the kiss when I draw my dying breath.

St. Joseph, head of the Holy Family and chaste spouse of the Blessed Virgin Mary, pray for us. (*Mention your intention here*)

Loving Father, You know that the deepest desire of my heart is to meet someone that I can share my life with. I trust in your loving plan for me and ask that I might meet soon the person that you have prepared for me. Through the power of your Holy Spirit, open my heart and mind so that I recognise my soulmate or better still lead him/her to me in your own unique way. Remove any obstacles that may be in the way of this happy encounter, so that I might find a new sense of wholeness, joy and peace. Give me the grace too, to know and accept, if you have another plan for my life. I surrender my past, present and future into the tender heart of your Son, Jesus, confident that my prayer will be heard and answered. Amen.

Memorare to St. Joseph

Remember, O most chaste spouse of the Virgin Mary, that never was it known that anyone who fled to you protection, implored your help, or sought your intercession was left unassisted. Full of confidence in

your power, I fly unto you and beg your protection. Despise not, O Guardian of the Redeemer, my humble supplication, but in your bounty, hear and answer me. Amen

Holy Cloak Novena of St. Joseph
(30 Days Prayer)

In the name of the Father, and the Son, and of the Holy Spirit, Amen

Jesus, Mary and Joseph, I give you my heart and my soul.

(Recite three Glory be to the Father, in thanksgiving for having exalted St Joseph to a position of such exceptional dignity).

Offering 1

O Glorious Patriarch St Joseph, I humbly prostrate myself before you. I beg the Lord Jesus, your Immaculate Spouse, the Blessed Virgin Mary, and all the angels and saints in the Heavenly Court, to join me in this devotion. I offer you this precious cloak, while pledging my sincerest faith and devotion. I promise to do all in my power to honour you throughout my lifetime to prove my love for you. Help me, St Joseph. Assist me now and throughout my lifetime, but especially at the moment of my death, as you were assisted by Jesus and Mary, that I may join you one day in Heaven and there honour you for all eternity. Amen

O Glorious Patriarch St Joseph, prostrate before you and your divine Son, Jesus, I offer you, with heartfelt devotion, this precious treasury of prayers, being ever mindful of the numerous virtues which adorned your sacred person. In you, O Glorious Patriarch, was fulfilled the dream of your precursor the first Joseph, who indeed seemed to have been sent by God to prepare the way for your presence on this earth. In fact, not only were you surrounded by the shining splendour of the rays of the divine Sun, Jesus, but you were splendidly reflected in the brilliant light of the mystic moon, the Blessed Virgin Mary. O Glorious Patriarch, if the example of the ancient Jacob, who personally went to congratulate his favorite son, who was exalted on the throne of Egypt, served to bring all his progeny there, should not the example of Jesus and Mary, who honoured you with their greatest respect and trust, serve to bring me, your devoted servant, to present you with this precious cloak in your honour. Grant, O Great St Joseph, that Almighty God may turn a benevolent glance toward me. As the ancient Joseph did not reject his guilty and cruel brothers, but rather accepted them with love and protected and saved them from hunger and death – I beseech you, O Glorious Patriarch, through your intercession, grant that the Lord may never abandon me in this exiled valley of sorrows. Grant that He may always number me as one of your devoted servants who live serenely under the patronage of your Holy Cloak. Grant that I may live always within the protection of this patronage, every day of my life and particularly at that moment when I draw my dying breath.

Prayers (I)

Hail O Glorious St Joseph, you who are entrusted with the priceless treasures of heaven and earth, and nurturer-father of Him who nourishes all creatures of the universe. You are, after Mary, the saint most worthy of our love and devotion. You alone, above all the saints, were chosen for that supreme honour of raising, guiding, nourishing and even embracing the Messiah, whom so many Kings and Prophets would have so desired to behold. St Joseph, save my soul and obtain for me from the Divine Mercy of God that petition for which I humbly pray. And for the holy souls in Purgatory, grant a great comfort from their pain.

Glory be to the Father… (3x)

Prayers (II)

O Powerful St Joseph, you were proclaimed the Patron of the Universal Church, therefore, I invoke you, above all the other saints, as the greatest protector of the afflicted, and I offer countless blessings to your most generous heart, always ready to help in any need. To you, O Glorious St Joseph, come the widows, the orphans, the abandoned, the afflicted, the oppressed. There is no sorrow, heartache or anguish which you have not consoled. Deign, I beseech you, to use on my behalf those gifts which God has given you, until I too shall be granted the answer to my petition. And you, holy souls in Purgatory, pray to St Joseph for me.

Glory be to the Father... (3x)

Prayers (III)

Countless are those who have prayed to you before me and have received comfort and peace, graces and favours. My heart, so sad and sorrowful, cannot find rest in the midst of this trial which besets me. O Glorious St Joseph, you know all my needs even before I set them forth in prayer. You know how important this petition is for me. I prostrate myself before you as I sigh under the heavy weight of the problem which confronts me. There is no human heart in which I can confide my sorrow; and even if I should find a compassionate creature who would be willing to assist me, still he would be unable to help me. Only you can help me in my sorrow, St Joseph, and I beg you to hear my plea. Has not St Theresa left it written in her dialogues – that the world may always know – "Whatever you ask of St Joseph, you shall receive." O St Joseph, comforter of the afflicted, have pity on my sorrow and pity on those poor souls who place so much hope in their prayers to you.

Glory be to the Father... (3x)

Prayers (IV)

O Sublime Patriarch St Joseph, because of your perfect obedience to God, you may intercede for me.

For your holy life full of grace and merit, hear my prayer. For your most sweet name, help me. For your most holy tears, comfort me. For your seven sorrows, intercede for me. For your seven joys, console me. From all harm of body and soul, deliver me. From all dangers and disaster, save me. Assist me with your powerful intercession and seek for me, through your power and mercy, all that is necessary for my salvation and particularly the favour of which I now stand in such great need.

Glory be to the Father… (3x)

Prayers (V)

O Glorious St Joseph, countless are the graces and favours which you have obtained for afflicted souls. Illness of every nature, those who are oppressed, persecuted, betrayed, bereft of all human comfort, even those in need of their life bread – all who implore your powerful intercession are comforted in their affliction. Do not permit, O dearest St Joseph, that I alone be the only one of all who have appealed to you, to be denied this petition which I so earnestly beg of you. Show your kindness and generosity even to me, that I may cry out in thanksgiving, "Eternal glory to our Holy Patriarch St Joseph, my great protector on Earth and the defender of the Holy Souls in Purgatory."

Glory be to the Father… (3x)

Prayers (VI)

Eternal Father, who are in Heaven, through the merits of Jesus and Mary, I beg you to grant my petition. In the name of Jesus and Mary I prostrate myself before your divine presence and I beseech you to accept my hopeful plea to persevere in my prayers that I may be numbered among the throngs of those who live under the patronage of St Joseph. Extend your blessing on this precious treasury of prayers which I today offer to him as a pledge of my devotion.

Glory be to the Father… (3x)

Supplications in Honor of St. Joseph's Hidden Life with Mary and Jesus

St Joseph, pray that Jesus may come into my soul and sanctify me.

St Joseph, pray that Jesus may come into my heart and inspire it with charity.

St Joseph, pray that Jesus may come into my mind and enlighten it.

St Joseph, pray that Jesus may guide my will and strengthen it.

St Joseph, pray that Jesus may direct my thoughts and purify them.

St Joseph, pray that Jesus may guide my desires and direct them.

St Joseph, pray that Jesus may look upon my deeds and extend his blessings.

St Joseph, pray that Jesus may inflame me with love for him.

St Joseph, request for me from Jesus the imitation of your virtues.

St Joseph, request for me from Jesus true humility of spirit.

St Joseph, request for me from Jesus meekness of heart.

St Joseph, request for me from Jesus peace of soul.

St Joseph, request for me from Jesus a holy fear of the Lord.

St Joseph, request for me from Jesus a desire for perfection.

St Joseph, request for me from Jesus a gentleness of heart.

St Joseph, request for me from Jesus a holy acceptance of suffering.

St Joseph, request for me from Jesus the wisdom of faith.

St Joseph, request for me from Jesus his blessing of perseverance in my good deeds.

St Joseph, request for me from Jesus the strength to carry my crosses.

St Joseph, request for me from Jesus a disdain for the material goods of this world.

St Joseph, request for me from Jesus the grace to always walk on the narrow path towards Heaven.

St Joseph, request for me from Jesus the grace to avoid all occasion of sin.

St Joseph, request for me from Jesus a holy desire for eternal bliss.

St Joseph, request for me from Jesus the grace of final perseverance.

St Joseph, do not abandon me.

St Joseph, pray that my heart may never cease to love you and that my lips may ever praise you.

St Joseph, for the love you bore for Jesus, grant that I may learn to love him.

St Joseph, graciously accept me as your devoted servant.

St Joseph, I give myself to you; accept my pleas and hear my prayers.

St Joseph, do not abandon me at the hour of my death.

Jesus, Mary and Joseph, I give you my heart and my Soul.

Glory be to the Father… (3x)

Invocations to St. Joseph

I)   Remember O most chaste spouse of the Blessed Virgin Mary, my good protector St Joseph, that never was it known that anyone who came to your protection, and sought your intercession was left unaided. Confidently, I prostrate myself before you and fervently beg for your powerful intervention. O Guardian of the Redeemer, despise not my petition, but in your mercy, hear and answer me. Amen

II) Glorious St Joseph, spouse of the Blessed Virgin Mary and virginal father of Jesus, look upon me and watch over me; lead me on the path of sanctifying grace; take heed of the urgent needs which I now beg you to envelop within the folds of your fatherly cloak. Dismiss those obstacles and difficulties standing in the way of my prayer and grant that the happy answer to my petition may serve for the greater glory of God and my eternal salvation. As a pledge of my undying gratitude, I promise to spread the word of your glory while offering thanks to the Lord for having so blessed your power and might in heaven and earth.

Litany of St. Joseph

Lord, have mercy.	Lord, have mercy.
Christ, have mercy.	Christ, have mercy.
Lord, have mercy.	Lord, have mercy.
Christ, hear us.	Christ, graciously hear us.
God, the Father of Heaven,	Have mercy on us.
God, the Son, Redeemer of the world,	Have mercy on us.
God, the Holy Spirit,	Have mercy on us.
Holy Trinity, One God,	Have mercy on us.
Holy Mary,	pray for us.
St. Joseph,	pray for us.
Noble son of David,	pray for us.
Light of Patriarchs,	pray for us.
Husband of the Mother of God,	pray for us.
Guardian of the Redeemer	pray for us.
Chaste Guardian of the Virgin	pray for us.
Nurturer of the Son of God	pray for us.
Zealous Defender of Christ	pray for us.

Servant of Christ	pray for us.
Minister of Salvation	pray for us.
Head of the Holy Family	pray for us.
Joseph most just	pray for us.
Joseph most chaste	pray for us
Joseph most prudent	pray for us.
Joseph most brave	pray for us.
Joseph most obedient	pray for us.
Joseph most faithful	pray for us
Mirror of patience	pray for us.
Lover of poverty	pray for us.
Model of Workers	pray for us.
Glory of Family Life	pray for us.
Guardian of Virgins	pray for us.
Pillar of families	pray for us.
Support in difficulties	pray for us.
Comfort of the Troubled	pray for us.
Hope of the Sick	pray for us.
Patron of Exiles	pray for us.
Patron of the Afflicted	pray for us.
Patron of the Poor	pray for us.
Patron of the Dying	pray for us.
Terror of demons	pray for us.
Protector of Holy Church,	pray for us.

Lamb of God, who takes away the sins of the world, spare us, O Lord

Lamb of God, who takes away the sins of the world, hear us, O Lord

Lamb of God, who takes away the sins of the world, have mercy on us

He made him the lord of his household

- And prince over all his possessions.

Let us Pray:

O God, in your ineffable providence you were pleased to choose Blessed Joseph to be the husband of your most holy Mother; grant, we beg you, that we may be worthy to have him for our intercessor in heaven whom on earth we venerate as our Protector: You who live and reign forever and ever. Amen.

Closing Prayer of the Holy Cloak

O Glorious Patriarch St Joseph, you who were chosen by God above all men to be the earthly head of the most holy of families, I beseech you to accept me within the folds of your Holy Cloak, that you may become the guardian and custodian of my soul. From this moment on, I choose you as my father, my protector, my counsellor, my patron and I beseech you to place in your custody my body, soul, all that I am, all that I possess, my life and my death. Look upon me as one of your children; defend me from the treachery of my enemies, invisible or otherwise, assist me at all times in all my necessities; console me in the bitterness of my life, and especially at the hour of my death. Say but one word for me to the divine Redeemer whom you were deemed worthy to hold in your arms, and to the Blessed Virgin Mary, your most chaste spouse. Request for me those blessings which will lead me to salvation. Include me among those who are most dear to you and I shall set forth to prove myself worthy of your special patronage. Amen

<u>Thirty Days Prayer to St. Joseph</u> (In Honour of the 30 Years He Spent with Jesus and Mary)

Ever blessed and glorious Joseph, kind and loving father, and helpful friend of all in sorrow! You are the good father and protector of orphans, the defender of the defenseless, the patron of those in need and sorrow.

Look kindly on my request. My sins have drawn down on me the just displeasure of my God, and so I am surrounded with unhappiness. To you, loving guardian of the Family of Nazareth, do I go for help and protection. Listen, then, I beg you, with fatherly concern, to my earnest prayers, and obtain for me the favours I ask.

I ask it by the infinite mercy of the eternal Son of God, which moved Him to take our nature and to be born into this world of sorrow.

I ask it by the weariness and suffering you endured when you found no shelter at the inn of Bethlehem

for the Holy Virgin, nor a house where the Son of God could be born. Then, being everywhere refused, you had to allow the Queen of Heaven to give birth to the world's Redeemer in a cave.

I ask it by the loveliness and power of that sacred Name, Jesus, which you conferred on the adorable Infant.

I ask it by the painful torture you felt at the prophecy of holy Simeon, which declared the Child Jesus and His Holy Mother future victims of our sins and of their great love for us.

I ask it through your sorrow and pain of soul when the angel declared to you that the life of the Child Jesus was sought by His enemies. From their evil plan, you had to flee with Him and His Blessed Mother to Egypt.

I ask it by all the suffering, weariness, and labors of that long and dangerous journey.

I ask it by all your care to protect the Sacred Child and His Immaculate Mother during your second journey, when you were ordered to return to your own country.

I ask it by your peaceful life in Nazareth where you met with so many joys and sorrows.

I ask it by your great distress when the adorable Child was lost to you and His mother for three days.

I ask it by your joy at finding Him in the temple, and by the comfort you found at Nazareth, while living in the company of the Child Jesus.

I ask it by the wonderful submission He showed in His obedience to you.

I ask it by the perfect love and conformity you showed in accepting the Divine order to depart from this life, and from the company of Jesus and Mary.

I ask it by the joy which filled your soul, when the Redeemer of the world, triumphant over death and hell, entered into the possession of His kingdom and led you into it with special honours.

I ask it through Mary's glorious Assumption, and through that endless happiness you have with her in the presence of God. O good father! I beg you, by all your sufferings, sorrows, and joys, to hear me and obtain for me what I ask.

(pause, mention your intentions)

Obtain for all those who have asked my prayers everything that is useful to them in the plan of God. Finally, my dear patron and father, be with me and all who are dear to me in our last moments, that we may eternally sing the praises of: JESUS, MARY AND JOSEPH.

"A blameless life, St. Joseph, may we lead, by your kind patronage from danger freed."

Seven Supplications to St. Joseph
(Translated from Italian)

I.   Most amiable St. Joseph, for the honour that the Eternal Father granted you by raising you to take his place on earth alongside his Most Holy Son Jesus, becoming his earthly father, obtain from God the grace I ask of you.

Glory be to the Father….

Saint Joseph, virginal father of Jesus, pray for me.

II.   Most amiable Saint Joseph, for the love that Jesus brought you, recognizing you as a tender father and obeying you as a respectful Son, implore for me from God the grace that I ask of you.

Glory be to the Father….

Saint Joseph, virginal father of Jesus, pray for me.

III.   Most pure St. Joseph, by the very special grace that you received from the Holy Spirit when he gave you his Bride, our dearest Mother, to marry you, obtain for me the grace so desired from God.

Glory be to the Father….

Saint Joseph, virginal father of Jesus, pray for me.

IV.   Most tender Saint Joseph, for the most pure love with which you loved Jesus as your Son and God, and Mary as your beloved bride, pray to the Most High God to grant me the grace for which I beg you.

Glory be to the Father....

Saint Joseph, virginal father of Jesus, pray for me.

V.   Most sweet St. Joseph, for the great joy that your heart felt in conversing with Jesus and Mary and in giving them your services, implore for me the most merciful God for the grace I so desire.

Glory be to the Father....

Saint Joseph, virginal father of Jesus, pray for me.

VI.   Most fortunate St. Joseph, for the beautiful privilege you had of dying in the arms of Jesus and Mary, and of being comforted in your agony by their presence, obtain for me from God, through your powerful intercession, the grace of which I so much stand in need.

Glory be to the Father....

Saint Joseph, virginal father of Jesus, pray for me.

VII. Most glorious St. Joseph, for the reverence that the whole celestial Court has for you as Nurturer father of Jesus and Spouse of Mary, hear my petitions that I present to you with lively faith, obtain for me the grace I so desire. Glory be to the Father....

Pray for us, St. Joseph, that we may be made worthy of the promises of Christ.

Let us pray:
O God, who in your inexpressible providence were pleased to choose Saint Joseph as spouse of the most holy Mother of your Son, grant, we pray, that we, who revere him as our protector on earth, may be worthy of his heavenly intercession. Through our Lord Jesus Christ, your Son, who lives and reigns with you in the unity of the Holy Spirit, God, forever and ever

Praise of St. Joseph (by St. John Eudes)
Hail, Joseph, image of God the Father,
Hail, Joseph, father of God the Son,
Hail, Joseph, temple of the Holy Spirit,
Hail, Joseph, beloved of the Most Holy Trinity,
Hail, Joseph, most faithful coadjutor of the great counsel,
Hail, Joseph, most worthy spouse of the Virgin Mary,
Hail, Joseph, father of all the faithful,
Hail, Joseph, guardian of all those who have embraced holy virginity,
Hail, Joseph, faithful observer of holy silence,
Hail, Joseph, lover of holy poverty,
Hail, Joseph, model of meekness and patience,
Hail, Joseph, mirror of humility and obedience;
Blessed art thou above all men,
Blessed thy eyes, which have seen the things which thou hast seen,
Blessed thy ears, which have heard the things thou hast heard,
Blessed thy hands, which have touched and handled

the Incarnate Word,
Blessed thy arms, which have borne him who bears
all things,
Blessed thy bosom, on which the Son of God
fondly rested,
Blessed thy heart, inflamed with burning love,
Blessed be the Eternal Father, who chose thee,
Blessed be the Son, who loved thee,
Blessed be the Holy Spirit, who sanctified thee,
Blessed be Mary, thy spouse, who cherished thee as
spouse and brother,
Blessed be the angel who served thee as a guardian,
And blessed forever be all who love and bless thee.
Amen.

The First Nine Wednesdays Devotion (A Devotion Promulgated by the Pious Union of St. Joseph)

Every Wednesday is dedicated in a special way to St. Joseph. Make the First Nine Wednesdays [in a manner similar to the Nine First Fridays of the Sacred Heart] in honour of St. Joseph for a happy death, for yourself and your dear ones. As charity is one of the best ways to be worthy of the grace of a happy death, offer your First Wednesday Mass and Communion and devotions in honour of St. Joseph in a special way for the salvation of the dying, most especially for an unrepentant sinner who is to lose his/her soul without the grace of final repentance.

Our Lord permits St. Joseph to take from His Divine treasury with full hands in order to give souls the

treasures of Divine grace and mercy, like Joseph, the son of Jacob, who took corn from the granaries of the King of Egypt to feed his brethren and all who had recourse to him. From the heights of Heaven, the King of Glory speaks to us the same words as Pharaoh spoke to the starving people of Egypt: "Go to Joseph."

The Go to Joseph Prayers

I

In the miseries of this vale of tears, to whom shall we have recourse, O blessed Joseph, if not to thee, to whom thy beloved spouse Mary entrusted all her rich treasures, that thou might keep them to our advantage? "Go to my spouse, Joseph," Mary seems to say to us, "and he will comfort you, he will deliver you from the misfortunes which now oppress you and will make you happy and contented" Have pity on us, therefore, O St. Joseph; have pity on us through that love which thou didst cherish toward a spouse so worthy and amiable.

Our Father... Hail Mary ... Glory Be ...

II

We are fully conscious that we have offended the justice of God by our sins and deserve His most severe chastisements. Now what shall be our place of refuge? "Go to Joseph," Jesus seems to say to us; "Go to Joseph, in whom I was well pleased and whom I had for My nurturing father. To him, as to a father, I have communicated all power, that he may use it for your good according to his own desire." Pity us, therefore, O blessed Joseph, pity us, for the great love thou didst bear toward a Son so admirable and so dear.

Our Father... Hail Mary ... Glory Be ...

III

Unhappily the sins we have committed call down upon the heaviest scourges: this we must confess. In what ark shall we take refuge in order to be saved? Where shall we find the blessed rainbow that shall give us comfort and hope in the midst of our afflictions? "Go to Joseph," the Eternal father seems to say to us: "Go to him who took My place on earth with regard to My Son made man. I entrusted to his keeping My Son, who is the unfailing source of grace; therefore, every grace is in his hands." Pity us, then, dear St. Joseph, pity us by thy great love for Almighty God, Who has been so generous to thee.

Our Father... Hail Mary ... Glory Be ...

Act of Consecration to St. Joseph

To your Chaste Heart we consecrate ourselves, on this day, O Glorious Saint Joseph. We consecrate our families and all that we have. Just as you protect Jesus and Mary, protect my soul and my life also, O our Beloved Protector, against the dangers that surround us and attack us. O Glorious Saint Joseph, teach us to love deeply the most Holy Hearts of Jesus and Mary, so that we may come to love deeply as they your Most

Chaste Heart, honoring it and making it known, as you deserve and ought to be Honoured and loved for all eternity. Amen!

Devotion to the Chaste Heart of St. Joseph

By José Rodrigues, Author of *The Book Of Joseph*

Did you know that the First Wednesday of every month is dedicated in devotion to the Most Chaste Heart of St. Joseph and it comes from Church-approved apparitions in Itapiranga, Brazil and the United States? The apparitions were approved by a Bishop Dom Carillo Gritti in 2010 and the Feast is usually celebrated on the first Wednesday after the Feast of the Sacred Heart of Jesus.

Conditions for Devotion:

Confession: This confession can be made 9 days before or after the First Wednesday, provided that Holy Communion be received in the state of grace.

Holy Communion: Offer your First Wednesday Mass and Communion in honor of St. Joseph, for the salvation of the dying, most especially for a hardened sinner who is to lose his soul without the grace of final repentance.

Prayer to the Chaste Heart of St. Joseph

Hail, Most Chaste Heart of St. Joseph, beating with love for the God who created you! Hail, Virginal Heart, lover of the Immaculate Heart of Mary! Hail, Paternal Heart, whose beating comforts the Sacred Heart of Jesus! Hail, you who are the Reflection of

God the Father, Guardian of God the Son, Friend of God the Holy Spirit, and Spouse of the Immaculate Handmaiden!

Most Chaste Heart of St. Joseph, beloved by God and His angels, I consecrate myself this day to your honour! In you I confide my joys and my sorrows, my pains and my pleasures. I know that you are always delighted to pour forth your graces to those who ask for them with confidence.

Therefore, confident in your goodness, I entrust myself, and the following person(s) to your care (*mention their names*). I ask that you please grant us the graces we need in order to become faithful reflections of you. I pray that you shower upon us all the graces necessary for our spiritual and temporal welfare. And I pray that you grant the Holy Catholic Church, our Mother, every available grace to bring about her glorious triumph! All for love of the two greatest treasures entrusted to your care: The Sacred Heart of Jesus and the Immaculate Heart of Mary. Amen.

CONSECRATION TO ST. JOSEPH

The consecration method adopted in this book follows the thirty-three (33) days consecration programme prepared by Fr. Donald Calloway, MIC, in his book *Consecration to St. Joseph*. The book by Fr. Calloway is indeed of immense benefit in knowing more about St. Joseph. It draws from the long tradition of devotion to St. Joseph in the Church and in a beautiful manner presents in a summary way the study of St. Joseph as reflected in the wisdom of Saints, the teachings of Popes and reflections of theologians. It exposes Josephology in a new way, tapping into the richness of the various titles in the litany of St. Joseph and supporting each with what he called "The Wonders of Our Spiritual Father". The book *Consecration to St. Joseph* is a must have for anyone willing to know more about St Joseph in this time and age and it is central to the Consecration to St. Joseph promoted here. It is beneficial to people in all works of life and opens up new horizons of thoughts for those who may intend to deepen their knowledge on St. Joseph our spiritual father. A copy is recommended for all who wish to participate in the thirty-three days preparation of consecration to St. Joseph.

Guide for the Day of Consecration

<u>Day of Consecration</u>

▶ The Consecration could take place within the celebration of the Holy Mass or outside of it, before the Tabernacle or a Statue of St. Joseph, with lighted candle in hand or well placed before the one who makes the act of consecration (a lily flower or any live flower can also be used).

▶ The consecration takes place after the homily, if within the Mass or following the "Prayer after Communion", as may be decided by the Priest. Those to be consecrated read the formula for consecration aloud together, mentioning their names where appropriate.

▶ The Priest blesses the medals of St. Joseph and helps them to wear it.

▶ At the end of the consecration they sign the formula and have their witness sign it at an appropriate time and keep the signed copy personally. They sing together a song to St. Joseph. The Priest congratulates the newly consecrated and blesses them.

▶ The Candles and/or flowers used for consecration may be left before the statue of St. Joseph if possible or taken away by the newly consecrated.

Act of Consecration to St. Joseph
(To be hand written)

For those already consecrated to the Blessed Virgin Mary

O Glorious Patriarch and Patron of the Church! O Virgin Spouse of the Virgin Mother of God! O Guardian and Virginal Father of the Word Incarnate! In the presence of Jesus and Mary, I _______________ choose you this day to be my father, my guardian, and my protector.

O great St. Joseph, whom God has made the Head of the Holy Family, accept me, I beseech you, though utterly unworthy, to be a member of your "Holy House." Present me to your Immaculate Spouse; to whom I am already consecrated. With her, pray that I may constantly think of Jesus, and serve him faithfully to the end of my life. O Terror of Demons, increase in me virtue, protect me from the evil one, and help me not to offend God in any way.

O my Spiritual Father, I hereby consecrate myself to you. In faithful imitation of Jesus and Mary, I place myself and all my concerns under your care and protection. To you, after Jesus and Mary, I consecrate my body and soul, with all their faculties, my spiritual growth, my home, and all my affairs and undertakings. Forsake me not, but adopt me as a servant and child of the Holy Family. Watch over me at all times, but especially at the hour of my death.

Console and strengthen me with the presence of Jesus and Mary so that, with you, I may praise and adore the Holy Trinity for all eternity. Amen.

Names: Date:

Signature

Witness: _________________
          Spiritual Guide

Act of Consecration to St. Joseph
(To be hand written)

For those who are yet to be consecrated to the Blessed Virgin Mary

O Glorious Patriarch and Patron of the Church! O Virgin Spouse of the Virgin Mother of God! O Guardian and Virginal Father of the Word Incarnate! In the presence of Jesus and Mary, I _______________ choose you this day to be my father, my guardian, and my protector.

O great St. Joseph, whom God has made the Head of the Holy Family, accept me, I beseech you, though utterly unworthy, to be a member of your "Holy House." Present me to your Immaculate Spouse and ask her also to adopt me as her child. With her, pray that I may constantly think of Jesus, and serve him faithfully to the end of my life. O Terror of Demons, increase in me virtue, protect me from the evil one, and help me not to offend God in any way.

O my Spiritual Father, I hereby consecrate myself to you. In faithful imitation of Jesus and Mary, I place myself and all my concerns under your care and protection. To you, after Jesus and Mary, I consecrate my body and soul, with all their faculties, my spiritual growth, my home, and all my affairs and undertakings. Forsake me not, but adopt me as a servant and child of the Holy Family. Watch over me at all times, but especially at the hour of my death. Console and strengthen me with the presence of Jesus and Mary so that, with you, I may praise and adore the Holy Trinity for all eternity. Amen.

Names: Date:

Signature

Witness: ______________________
                  Spiritual Guide

Concluding Prayer

Priest: God our Father, listen favourably to the prayer of your servant(s) who, this day, makes his/her (their) consecration to you through the hands of St. Joseph, the chosen instrument whom you made master of Your household and entrusted with the care of Jesus and Mary. Help him/her (them) in his/her (their) resolve to live virtuously in the imitation of the

Guardian of the Redeemer who today he/she (they) take(s) as a model of life, so that guided by him and his Immaculate Spouse, the Virgin Mary, he/she (they) may grow in grace, love, wisdom and holiness, and merit the joys of eternal life. Through our Lord Jesus Christ Your Son who lives and reigns with you in the unity of the Holy Spirit, God, forever and ever. Amen!

Consecration of the family to Saint Joseph

(To be done before a Statue or Image of St. Joseph)
Fr. Michael Odubela, OSJ

Priest greets all present and explains briefly the simple rite to be performed

Act of Consecration: O Glorious Patriarch and Patron of the Church! O Virgin Spouse of the Virgin Mother of God! O Guardian and Virginal Father of the Word Incarnate! In the presence of Jesus and Mary, we, the members of .... family, choose you this day to be our father, guardian, and protector. O great Saint Joseph, whom God has made the Head of the Holy Family, accept us, we beseech you, though utterly unworthy we are, to be members of your "Holy House." Present us to your Immaculate Spouse anew – (*if already consecrated to Mary*) **or** ask her also to adopt us as her children – (*if not yet consecrated to Mary*). With her, pray that we may constantly think of Jesus, and serve him faithfully to the end of our lives. O Terror of Demons, increase in us virtues, protect us from the evil one, and help us not to offend God in any way. O Spiritual Father, we hereby consecrate our family and all her members to you. In faithful imitation of Jesus and Mary, we place all our concerns under your care and protection. To you, after Jesus and Mary, we consecrate our bodies and souls, with all their faculties, our spiritual growth, our works (and studies), and all our affairs and undertakings. Forsake us not, but adopt us as servants and children of the Holy Family. Keep every evil away from our household and help us to find fulfillment in the plans of God for Us. Watch over us at all times, but especially at the hour of our death. Console and strengthen us with the presence of Jesus and Mary so that, with you, we may praise and adore the Holy Trinity for all eternity. Amen.

St. Joseph, Head of the Holy Family - Pray for us

St. Joseph, Head of the Holy Family – Keep unfailing watch over us

St. Joseph, Head of the Holy Family – Make our family holy, loving and peaceful. Amen

Litany of St. Joseph   **See page 16**

Concluding Prayer

To be said by a Priest

Jesus, Mary and Joseph, in your holy home at Nazareth we contemplate the splendor of true love and service. To you do we turn with trust and confidence, as we pray for the family of

…………………., whom we are consecrating to you, through the hands of St. Joseph, the Head of the Holy Family. Fill the hearts of each member of this family with zeal for the salvation of their soul and with charity to be builders of communion in their home, in the Church and wherever they may be. Give them the right disposition to be attentive to the needs of one another and to the call to love and service for one another, as you did. Help them to be humble and respectful towards one another and to seek always the good and interests of one another in all things. Help them to be docile to the promptings of the Holy Spirit as you were and to live in perfect conformity to the will of God. Help them to cultivate the virtues of patience, industry, diligence and sacrifice, and to have respect for all that the Lord commands. Banish the snares of evil from this home and from every one of her member and grant increase to your children in goodness. Unite them in your peace and strengthen their bond of love for one another, so that blessed by you they may remain unbroken in life and be united forever in the glory of God the Father in heaven. Amen!

Blessing: The Lord be with you

R/ And with your spirit

Through the intercession of Mary and Joseph, May Almighty God bless and keep you,

+   The Father, and the Son, and the Holy Spirit. Amen!

Go in the peace of Christ

R/ Thanks be to God!

Hymn to St. Joseph   **See page 174 - 181**

<u>Parents Prayer of Consecration of their Children to St. Joseph</u>

(Fr. Michael Odubela, OSJ)

O holy Patriarch, Saint Joseph, to you who watched over the Son of God entrusted to your care do we consecrate our children (*mention their names*), be their guide and safety as you were for Jesus. Preserve in them the grace of innocence and let the light of goodness shine forth always in them and through them. Keep them from all dangers to body and soul, and inspire constantly in them a tender love for you, for Mary your Immaculate Spouse, and for Jesus, your adorable Son. May your holy protection be with them all the days of their life. Watch over them and be their inspiration in the practice of all that is good, give guidance in every activity, conduct them always in the path of the precepts of the Lord, and deign to bring them at the end of their earthly pilgrimage, together with us, to the divine presence of God in Heaven, where united for all eternity we may sing the unending praises of God, through Christ our Lord. Amen.

Glory be to the Father 3X

Hymn to St. Joseph

VARIOUS ACTS OF CONSECRATION TO ST. JOSEPH

Act of Consecration to St. Joseph (Author Unknown)

Glorious Saint Joseph! Worthy amongst all the saints to be venerated, loved, and invoked, because of the excellence of thy virtues, eminence of thy glory, and the power of thy intercession. In the presence of the most Adorable and Holy Trinity, of Jesus Christ thy adopted Son, and of Mary thy chaste spouse and my tender Mother, I take thee this day as my advocate, my protector, and father. I firmly resolve never to forget thee, and to love and honour thee all the days of my life, and to do all that I can to spread devotion to thee among the faithful. Deign to protect me in a special manner, O my beloved father. I am not worthy, it is true; yet, in the name of the love thou bearest for Jesus and Mary, receive me among the number of thy special friends. In the name of this double society, which was formed beside thee by Jesus and Mary, protect me as long as I live, so that I may never be separated from God by sin. In the name of thy happy death, in the arms of Jesus and Mary, protect me, especially at the hour of my death; so that dying, accompanied by thee, by Jesus, and by Mary, I may come to thank thee in Heaven, and in thy holy company praise, bless, glorify, and enjoy God for all

eternity. Amen

Act of Consecration to St. Joseph (by St. Peter Julian Eymard)

I consecrate myself to you, good St. Joseph, as my spiritual father. I choose you to rule my soul and to teach me the interior life, the life hidden away with Jesus, Mary, and yourself. Above all, I want to imitate the humble silence with which you shrouded Jesus and Mary. For me everything lies in that — self-abnegation like our Lord in his hidden life, making the world forget me by my silence and my practice of virtue. I consecrate myself to you as my guide and model in all my duties so that I may learn to fulfill them with meekness and humility: with meekness toward my brethren, my neighbor, and all with whom I come in contact; with humility toward myself and simplicity before God. I choose you, good saint, as my counsellor, my confidant, my protector in all my difficulties and trials. I do not ask to be spared crosses and sufferings, but only from self-love which might take away their value by making me vain about them. I choose you as my protector. Be my father as you were the father of the Holy Family at Nazareth. Be my guide; be my protector. I do not ask for temporal goods, greatness, or power. I ask only that I serve with fidelity and devotedness my divine King. I shall honour, love, and serve you with Mary, my mother, and never shall I separate her name from yours. O Jesus, give me Joseph for a father as you have given me Mary as a mother. Fill me with devotion, confidence, and filial love. Listen to my prayer. I know that you will. Already I feel more devout, more full of hope and confidence in good St. Joseph, your virgin father and my spiritual father. Amen.

Act of Consecration to St. Joseph (by St. Alphonsus Liguori)

O Holy Patriarch, I rejoice with you at the exalted dignity by which you were deemed worthy to act as father to Jesus, to give him orders and to be obeyed by him whom heaven and earth obey. O great saint, as you were served by God, I too wish to be taken into your service. I choose you, after Mary, to be my chief advocate and protector. I promise to honour you every day by some special act of devotion and by placing myself under your daily protection. By that sweet company which Jesus and Mary gave you in your lifetime, protect me all through life, so that I may never separate myself from my God by losing his grace. My dear St. Joseph, pray to Jesus for me. Certainly, he can never refuse you anything, as he obeyed all your orders while on earth. Tell him to detach me from all creatures and from myself, to inflame me with his holy love, and then to do with me what he pleases. By that assistance which Jesus and Mary gave you at death, I beg of you to protect me in a special way at the hour of my death, so that dying assisted by you, in the company of Jesus and Mary, I may go to thank you in paradise and, in your company, to praise my God for all eternity. Amen.

Act of Consecration to St. Joseph (by St. Bernardine of Siena)

O my beloved St. Joseph, adopt me as thy child. Take charge of my salvation; watch over me day and night; preserve me from the occasions of sin; obtain for me purity of body. Through thy intercession with Jesus, grant me a spirit of sacrifice, humility, self-denial, burning love for Jesus in the Blessed Sacrament, and a sweet and tender love for Mary, my mother. Saint Joseph, be with me living, be with me dying, and obtain for me a favorable judgment from Jesus, my merciful Savior. Amen.

DAILY DEVOTION FOR CONSECRATED MEMBERS

In the name of the Father and of the Son and of the Holy Spirit. Amen

Morning Offering to St. Joseph

Receive me, dear and chosen father, glorious St. Joseph, and the offering of every movement of my body and soul, which I desire to present through thee to my blessed Lord. Purify all! Make all a perfect holocaust! May every pulsation of my heart be a Spiritual Communion, every look and thought an act of love, every action a sweet sacrifice, every word an arrow of Divine love, every step an advance towards Jesus, every visit to Our Lord as pleasing to God as the errands of Angels, every thought of thee, dear Saint, an act to remind thee that I am thy child. I recommend to thee the occasions in which I usually fail, particularly (*Mention those occasions and your habitual sins*). Accept each little devotion of the day, though replete with imperfection, and offer it to Jesus, whose mercy will overlook all, since He regards not so much the gift as the love of the giver. Amen.

Memorare to St. Joseph

Remember, O most chaste spouse of the Virgin Mary, that never was it known that anyone who fled to your protection, implored your help, or sought your intercession was left unassisted. Full of confidence in your power, I fly unto you and beg your protection. Despise not, O Guardian of the Redeemer, my humble supplication, but in your bounty, hear and answer me. Amen.

Or

Memorare to Mary and Joseph

Remember O Most Gracious Virgin Mary and St. Joseph that never was it known that anyone who fled to your protection, implored your help, or sought your intercession was left unaided. Inspired by this confidence, I come to you, O Virgin of Virgins, my mother, and you, Minister of Salvation, my spiritual father, sinful and sorrowful, O Mother of the Word Incarnate and you Guardian of the Redeemer despise not my petitions, but in your goodness and bounty, hear and answer me. Amen.

Daily Act of Consecration to St. Joseph

O dearest St. Joseph, I consecrate myself to your honour and give myself to you that you may always be my father, my protector, and my guide in the way of salvation. Obtain for me a greater purity of heart and a fervent love of the interior life. After your example, may I do all my actions for the greater glory of God, in union with the Sacred Heart of Jesus and the Immaculate Heart of Mary. O Blessed St. Joseph, pray for me that I may share in the peace and joy of your holy death. Amen.

Litany of St Joseph

Lord, have mercy.	Lord, have mercy.
Christ, have mercy.	Christ, have mercy.
Lord, have mercy.	Lord, have mercy.
Christ, hear us.	Christ, graciously hear us.
God, the Father of Heaven,	Have mercy on us.
God, the Son, Redeemer of the world,	Have mercy on us.
God, the Holy Spirit,	Have mercy on us.
Holy Trinity, One God,	Have mercy on us.
Holy Mary,	pray for us.
St. Joseph,	pray for us.
Noble son of David,	pray for us.
Light of Patriarchs,	pray for us.
Husband of the Mother of God,	pray for us.

Guardian of the Redeemer	pray for us.
Chaste Guardian of the Virgin	pray for us.
Nurturer of the Son of God	pray for us.
Zealous Defender of Christ	pray for us.
Servant of Christ	pray for us.
Minister of Salvation	pray for us.
Head of the Holy Family	pray for us.
Joseph most just	pray for us.
Joseph most chaste	pray for us.
Joseph most prudent	pray for us.
Joseph most brave	pray for us.
Joseph most obedient	pray for us.
Joseph most faithful	pray for us.
Mirror of patience	pray for us.
Lover of poverty	pray for us.
Model of Workers	pray for us.
Glory of Family Life	pray for us.
Guardian of Virgins	pray for us.
Pillar of families	pray for us.
Support in difficulties	pray for us.
Comfort of the Troubled	pray for us.
Hope of the Sick	pray for us.
Patron of Exiles	pray for us.
Patron of the Afflicted	pray for us.
Patron of the Poor	pray for us.
Patron of the Dying	pray for us.
Terror of demons	pray for us.
Protector of Holy Church,	pray for us.

Lamb of God, who takes away the sins of the world, spare us, O Lord.

Lamb of God, who takes away the sins of the world, graciously hear us, O Lord.

Lamb of God, who takes away the sins of the world, have mercy on us

He made him the lord of his household

- And prince over all his possessions.

Let us pray:

O God, in your ineffable providence you were pleased to choose Blessed Joseph to be the husband of your most holy Mother; grant, we beg you, that we may be worthy to have him for our intercessor in heaven whom on earth we venerate as our Protector: You who live and reign forever and ever. Amen.

Daily Rosary with the Mystery of the day or the Rosary of St. Joseph on Wednesdays

PRAYERS TO ST. JOSEPH AT VARIOUS TIMES AND FOR VARIOUS NEEDS

Prayer to St. Joseph For Faith

O Blessed St. Joseph, heir of all the Patriarchs, obtain for me this beautiful and precious virtue. Give me a lively faith, which is the foundation of all holiness, that faith without which no one can be pleasing to God. Obtain for me a faith that triumphs over all the temptations of the world and conquers human respects; a faith that cannot be shaken and that seeks God alone. In imitation of you, make me live by faith and submit my mind and heart to God, so that one day I may behold in Heaven what I now firmly believe on earth. Amen.

A Loving Prayer to St. Joseph

O St. Joseph, whose protection is so great, so strong and so prompt before the throne of God, I place to you all my interest and desires. O St. Joseph do assist me by your powerful intercession and obtain for me from the throne of your Divine Son, our Lord Jesus Christ, all the spiritual blessings so that having engaged here below your heavenly intercession I may offer my thanksgiving and homage to the eternal father. O St. Joseph I never grow tired contemplating you with Jesus asleep in your arms. I dare not approach as he reposes near your heart. Press him in my name and kiss his dear head for me and ask him to return the kisses when I draw my dying breath - Amen. O St. Joseph, hear my prayer and obtain my petitions. Amen. O St. Joseph pray for me. Amen.

Prayer to St. Joseph, Patron of the Church

Glorious Patriarch Saint Joseph! a voice of far greater authority than that which once issued from the throne of Egypt has lately directed the great Christian family to have recourse to thee in their necessities: Go to Joseph. Behold then this widely extended family entrusted to thy care; behold us all, prostrate before thy heavenly throne, imploring thy assistance in our present grievous afflictions. Like the brothers of the ancient Joseph, we come to thee, humbled and confounded on the account of our sins, which have called down upon us the anger of Heaven. Yet in our midst there are also many innocent Benjamins, who suffer and grieve without any fault of their own. But our hearts are inexpressibly pained when we hear our venerable Father, like the gentle and pious Jacob, meekly lamenting that the last days of his life are filled with bitterness. Have pity on his gray hairs, and permit him not to close his eyes in the sleep of the Just, before peace and safety have dawned upon his entire family. This, O great Saint, is the first favour which we ask of thee since thou hast been proclaimed our universal protector. Canst thou have the heart to refuse us? Ah! we may well hope that the second Joseph will show even greater compassion than the first. Animated therefore with this confidence, we repeat: Holy Joseph, Pray for Us.

Prayer for Priests and Religious

O glorious Saint Joseph, you who, on the word of the angel speaking to you in the night, did put fear aside to take your Virgin Bride into your home, show yourself today the advocate and protector of priests and religious. Guardian of the Infant Christ, defend them against every attack of the enemy, preserve them from the dangers that surround them on every side. Forget not Herod's threats against the Child Jesus, the anguish of the flight into Egypt by night, and the hardships of your exile. Stand by the accused; stretch out your hand to those who have fallen; comfort the fearful; forsake not the weak; and visit the lonely. Let all priests and religious know that, in you, God has given them a model of faith in the night, of obedience in adversity, of chastity in tenderness, and of hope in uncertainty. You are the terror of demons and the healer of those wounded in spiritual combat. Come, then, to the defence of every priest and religious in need; overcome evil with good. Where there are curses, put blessings, where harm has been done, do good. Let there be joy for the priests and religious of the Church, and peace for all under your gracious protection. Amen.

Prayer for a Particular Priest

O glorious Saint Joseph, I present to you this day Father N., priest of Jesus Christ, and beg you to be to him advocate and defender, counsellor and friend. Open your heart to him as you did open your home to the Virgin Mother in her hour of need. Protect his

holy priesthood as you did protect the life of the Infant Christ threatened by cruel Herod. In darkness bring him light; in weakness, strength; and in fear the peace that passes understanding. For the sake of the tender love that bound you to the Virgin Mary and to the Infant Christ, be for him, Saint Joseph, a constant intercessor and a shield against every danger of body, mind, and soul so that, in spite of his weaknesses and sins, his priesthood may bring glory to Christ and serve to increase the beauty of holiness in His bride, the Church. Amen.

Prayer to St. Joseph, Terror of Demons

Saint Joseph, Terror of Demons! Cast your solemn gaze upon the devil and all of his minions, and protect us with your mighty staff. You fled through the night to avoid the devil's wicked designs, now with the power of God smite the demons as they flee from you! Grant special protection, we pray, for children, fathers, families, and the dying. By God's grace no demon dares approach while you are near, so we beg of you, always be near to us, through Christ our Lord. Amen.

Prayer to St. Joseph for Protection

Great St. Joseph, you guided our Lord Jesus Christ from his childhood and He called you father. Humbly I beseech you, be a father to me, since Jesus has made you his father. You worked for Him and you taught Him to work. Teach me too. You kept Him safe in the

flight into Egypt, keep me safe in my journey through life. Let me never turn aside from the right road of the love of our Lord, and of faith and hope in Him. May I, as you did, have Jesus and Mary at my death-bed; and as you are, may I be united with Him forever in heaven. Amen

Daily Prayer to St. Joseph for Protection (By. Ven. Martin Von Cochem)

HAIL O SAINT JOSEPH! I, thine unworthy child, greet thee. Thou art the faithful protector and intercessor of all who love and venerate thee. Thou knowest that I have special confidence in thee and, after Jesus and Mary place all my hope of salvation in thee, for thou art all-powerful with God and will never abandon thy faithful servants. Therefore, I humbly invoke thee and commend myself, with all who are dear to me, and my entire possessions, to thy secure protection and powerful intercession. I beseech thee, by the love of Jesus and Mary, do not abandon me during life, and assist me at the hour of my death. Amen.

Prayer to St. Joseph to Obtain the Holy Virtue of Purity

O faithful guardian and father of virgins, glorious Saint Joseph, to whom was confided the care of Jesus and of Mary, the Queen of Virgins, I most humbly supplicate thee, by the love thou didst bear Jesus and Mary, to obtain for me that, being preserved from every stain during life, I may serve them with

unspotted purity of mind and body.

Prayer to St. Joseph for Guidance in the Choice of a Vocation

Great Saint, who was so docile to the leading of the Holy Spirit, obtain for me grace to know to what state Providence has destined me. Please do not permit me to err in this important choice, upon which depends my happiness in this world, and perhaps my eternal salvation, but obtain for me, that, enlightened concerning the Divine Will, and being faithful in following it, I may walk in the way that the Lord has determined for me, which will conduct me to a blessed eternity. Amen.

Prayer of Fathers to St. Joseph

Dear St. Joseph, you took the place of the Heavenly Father in respect of Jesus, the Son of God become human. You were a model father to Jesus and loved Him as your own son. Help me to be worthy of the name father, which belongs to the Father from all eternity and which he has been pleased to confer on me. May I always be for my children a source of life — corporal, intellectual and spiritual. Enable me to contribute in great part to their physical growth by my work, to their mental and spiritual growth by good schooling and to their supernatural life by my prayers and example, so that they may become complete human beings and true children of their Heavenly Father. Let me be ever conscious that my actions are

far more important than my words. May I give them a good example in all the situations of life. May I wear my successes modestly and my failures courageously. May I be temperate in time of joy and steadfast in time of sorrow. May I remain humble after doing good and contrite after doing evil. May I emulate our Heavenly Father, and scrupulously respect my children's rights as human persons and their freedom to follow a rightly formed conscience, while at the same time fulfilling my duty to guide them in the way given us by your Son Jesus Christ, to whom you were a most loving father all the days of your life. May I obtain the grace to be a similar father for my children. Amen.

A Parent's Thanksgiving Prayer for a Newborn Child

Saint Joseph, you witnessed the miracle of birth, seeing the infant Jesus born of your most holy spouse, the Virgin Mary. With wonder and awe, you took into your arms the Saviour. With gratitude that only a parent can know, you glorified God for the birth of His Son, entrusted to your fatherly care. Like you, St. Joseph, I too give praise and glory to God for the birth of my child. This child's life is such a miraculous testimony of God's loving presence. My heart is filled with grateful joy. Join with me, dear St. Joseph, in offering thanks to God for the gift of my child.

What great confidence God placed in you, St. Joseph, by entrusting his only Son to your fatherly care. This inspires me to entrust the spiritual care and protection of my newborn child into your competent and loving hands. Teach, guide, and support me to fulfill well my awesome vocation to be a worthy parent to this child. Amen.

Prayer to St. Joseph Protector of Homes

St. Joseph, protect our home. Pour forth from heaven blessings on our family. Remain in our midst. Help us to live in love and harmony, in peace and joy. May the wholesome fear of God strengthen us that virtue may adorn what we do and our way may lead to heaven. To you this day I give the key to our dwelling place. Lock out all things that could do us harm. Lock my home and my loved ones with me in the hearts of Jesus and Mary. This I beg of you, that our days may be like your days in the holy home at Nazareth. Amen.

Prayer of Spouses to St. Joseph

Dear St. Joseph, humble and just husband of Mary, grant us your powerful intercession that especially husbands and wives may be faithful to their sacred vows. Inspire them with the desire to be not only just but also charitable towards each other. In imitation of your behaviour, may we always endeavour to do God's will. Let us realise the great responsibility that is ours with respect to our partners, especially in what concerns our growth in holiness as willed by God. When we have children, let us realise that there is no greater good by us upon earth than to do our best in raising them as children of God, destined to live in perfect happiness with God for all eternity. May we follow your example and that of Mary, your spouse, and above all the example of the One Who lived so long with you and was the Son of God made Man. Amen.

Prayer to the Holy Family

Most loving Jesus, by your sublime and beautiful virtues and by the example of your family life you blessed with peace and happiness the family chosen by you on earth. Graciously look on this family humbly kneeling before you and imploring your mercy. Remember that we belong entirely to you, for it is to you we have in a special way dedicated and devoted ourselves. Look on us in your loving kindness, preserve us from dangers, and give us the grace to persevere to the end in the imitation of your holy family. After revering and loving you faithfully on earth, may we bless and praise you eternally in heaven. Mary, our dearest mother, to your intercession we have recourse, knowing that your divine Son will hear your prayers. Glorious Patriarch, St. Joseph, assist us by your powerful mediation, and offer by the hands of Mary our prayers to Jesus. Jesus, Mary, and Joseph, enlighten us, assist us, save us. Amen.

Prayer for Marriage and Family

Triune Lord of Life and Love, bless husbands and wives with the graces to be life-giving lovers and life-loving givers. As generous and responsible parents, who respect children as the most excellent fruit of marriage, may every marital embrace be free, total, faithful and open to new life. May the dark scourges of self-centered anxiety, contraception, sterilization, abortion, and every other sin against the sacred meaning of human sexuality, be vanquished by your healing Mercy, coupled with the graces to faithfully live the glorious beauty of your purpose for marriage and family, in the image of the Holy Family, Jesus, Mary, and Joseph, and in your own Image: Father, Son and Holy Spirit. Amen.

Prayer to St. Joseph for Vocations

St. Joseph, glorious patron of the Church, we ask you to intercede before God so that, in our days, as always in the Church, many young people may be attracted to the service of souls and to the ideals of evangelical perfection. Among Christian nations, the faithful desire to better understand and practise the virtues preached by Christ; and among non-Christian peoples, many a great number of men and women of good will, hear the call of faith and want to receive the message of peace. Please pray on our behalf that the Lord of the harvest will send workers to his vineyard. Obtain for us many good priestly and religious vocations that respond to the immense needs of the world today and that are fully dedicated to the service

of the Lord and of the Church. Amen.

Prayer to St. Joseph before Work (by Pope St. Pius X)

O Glorious Saint Joseph, model of all workers, obtain for me the grace to work in a spirit of penance for the expiation of my many sins; to work conscientiously, putting the call of duty above my natural inclinations; to work with thankfulness and joy, considering it an honour to employ and develop by means of labour the gifts received from God; to work with order, peace, moderation, and patience, never shrinking from weariness and trials; to work above all with purity of intention and detachment from self, keeping unceasingly before my eyes death and the account that I must give of time lost, talents unused, good omitted, and vain complacency in success, so fatal to the work of God. All for Jesus, all through Mary, all after thy example, O Patriarch, Saint Joseph. Such shall be my watchword in life and in death. Amen.

Prayer for Workers

O glorious Saint Joseph, who, under the humble appearance of a workman, have hidden your unique and royal dignity of guardian of Jesus and Mary, and by your toil have supported them, protect in your love and power the workers who are specially entrusted to you. You know their anxieties and sufferings, because you have undergone them yourself, with Jesus and Mary at your side. Do not permit that, laden with the cares of the world, they forget the end for which they have been created by God; do not let seeds of mistrust get hold of their immortal souls. Recall to all workers in the fields, schools, offices, factories, mines, markets and laboratories that they are not isolated in their work, in their joys and in their trials, but that Jesus and Mary, his mother and ours, are standing beside them to support them, to wipe their sweat and bless their fatigue. Teach them to change their labour into a means of high sanctification as you did. Amen.

V: Glory be to the Father, and to the Son, and to the Holy Spirit:

R: As it was in the beginning, is now, and ever shall be, world without end. Amen.

V: St. Joseph our protector,

R: Pray for us.

Prayer for one Seeking Employment

Dear Saint Joseph, you were yourself once faced with the responsibility of providing the necessities of life for Jesus and Mary. Look down with fatherly compassion upon me in my anxiety over my present inability to support my family. Please help me to find gainful employment very soon, so that this heavy burden of concern will be lifted from my heart and that I will soon be able to provide for those whom God has entrusted to my care. Help us to guard against bitterness and discouragement, so that we may emerge from this trial spiritually enriched and with even greater blessings from God. Amen

Prayer for the Unemployed

O St. Joseph, we pray to you for those who are out of work, for those who want to earn their living and support their families. You who are the patron of workers; grant that unemployment may vanish from our ranks, that all those who are ready to work may put their strength and abilities into serving their fellow men and earn a just salary. You are the patron of families; do not let those who have children to support and raise, lack the necessary means. Have pity on our brothers and sisters held down in unemployment and poverty because of sickness or social disorders. Help our political leaders and captains of industry find new and just solutions: may each and every one have the joy of contributing, according to his abilities, to the common prosperity. Grant that we may all share together in the abundant good God has given and that we may help the under privileged ones. Amen.

Prayer to St. Joseph to Obtain Spiritual Grace

Great Saint Joseph, who are the director, the friend, and the protector of those souls who desire to be perfect, thou who didst learn from Jesus and Mary how to conquer the powers of hell, and to practise all virtues, obtain for me (specify the grace you wish to receive). Beloved Saint, my father, my guide, and my model, thou who hast so much zeal for the glory of Jesus Christ, and for my sanctification, canst thou reject my petition? No, I have the sweet confidence

that thou wilt not reject it. Thy goodness will supply that which is lacking in my fervour, and according to the depth of thy love for me, and of thy power with Him Who has deigned to be called thy Son, thou wilt favourably hear me. Amen

A Prayer to St. Joseph for all Needful Graces

O blessed Joseph, since Jesus while on Earth was subject to thee, rendered prompt obedience to thy commands, and cherished thee with most especial love and honor, how shall He now refuse thee anything in Heaven, where all thy merits receive their full reward! Pray for me therefore, O holy Patriarch, and obtain for me those necessary graces: first of all, that I may have a sincere contrition for my sins, that I may ever hate and fear all that is evil, and fly from it with firmness and constancy, especially from my most besetting sins; secondly, that I may amend my life daily more and more, and constantly apply myself to the acquirement of virtues, especially those virtues which I need most; and lastly, that I may be kept safe amidst the various temptations and occasions, by which my soul may be exposed to the peril of damnation. For these and all other needful graces, O holy Joseph, I commend myself to the goodness and mercy of my God, and to thy fatherly care and intercession. Amen.

Miraculous Prayer to St. Joseph

"Glorious St. Joseph, guardian and Protector of Jesus Christ! To you I raise my heart and my hands to implore your powerful intercession. Please obtain for me from the kind heart of Jesus the help and the graces necessary for my spiritual and temporal welfare. I ask particularly for the grace of a happy death and the special favour I now implore. *Mention your request here.* Guardian of the Word incarnate, I feel animated with confidence that your prayers on my behalf will graciously be heard before the throne of God. O glorious St. Joseph, through the love you bear to Jesus Christ, and for the glory of His Name. Hear my prayers and obtain my petitions. Amen."

Prayer to St. Joseph to Obtain the Conversion of a Sinner

O holy Joseph, I earnestly recommend to thy care the salvation of the soul of N., which Jesus has redeemed by the shedding of His Blood. Thou knowest, great saint, how miserable are those who have banished this Divine Saviour from their hearts, and are in danger of eternally losing Him. Do not permit, then, that this soul so dear to me may be longer separated from Him; enlighten it with regard to the dangers that threaten it. Powerfully move this heart, and bring back this prodigal child to the bosom of the best of Fathers. Do not abandon it until thou hast opened to it the gates of Heaven, where it will bless thee eternally for the happiness which thou hast procured for it. Amen.

Prayer for a Happy Death

O Blessed St. Joseph, you gave forth your last breath in the loving embrace of Jesus and Mary. When the

seal of death shall close my life, please come with Jesus and Mary to aid me. Obtain for me this solace for the hour: to die with their holy arms around me. Jesus, Mary and Joseph, I commend my soul unto your sacred arms. Amen.

℣. Pray for us... O most blessed Joseph,

℟. that we may be made worthy of the promises of Christ.

Prayer in Honour of St. Joseph for the Dying

Eternal Father, by thy love for Saint Joseph, whom Thou didst select from among all men to represent Thee upon Earth, have mercy on us and on the dying.

Our Father ... Hail Mary ... Glory Be ...

Eternal divine Son, by Thy love of Saint Joseph, who was Thy faithful guardian upon Earth, have mercy on us and on the dying.

Our Father ... Hail Mary ... Glory Be ...

Eternal divine Spirit, by Thy love for Saint Joseph, Who so carefully watched over Mary, Thy beloved spouse, have mercy on us and on the dying.

Our Father ... Hail Mary ... Glory Be ...

A Parent's Prayer Entrusting a Deceased Child

St. Joseph, after your most holy spouse, our Blessed Mother, you were the first to take into your arms and heart the baby Jesus. From the first time you gazed upon him and held him, your heart and soul were

forever bonded to him. You caressed the Holy Child with fatherly love and affection, and you committed yourself always to love, protect, and care for this Son. Look now with similar love and affection upon this child of mine, who has gone from this world. I place my child, as well as my grief and guilt, into the eternal embrace of your arms. Hold and caress my child for me with the love of my arms and sweetly kiss my child with all the tender affection of my heart. As God the Father entrusted the care of His most precious Son into your most loving and confident hands, so too do I entrust into your fatherly care this child of mine. Please present him to the merciful hands of Our Lord, so that one day, when I too leave this world, my child may greet me into eternal life. Amen.

Prayer to St. Joseph for a Soul in Purgatory

Great Saint Joseph, who so tenderly loved Jesus, I earnestly recommend to thee the soul of N., who may at this moment be suffering in purgatory. Be thou his/her consoler in that place of suffering and expiation! Deign to apply to him/her the pious suffrages of the faithful, particularly my own, and be thou his/her intercessor with Jesus and with Mary. Obtain by thy prayers that, delivered from the bonds that hold him in captivity, he may fly to the bosom of God, there to be eternally in the enjoyment of those delights with which the elect are blessed. Amen.

FEASTS OF ST. JOSEPH

The pioneer Pope on recognition of St. Joseph's feast was Pope Sixtus IV (1471 - 1484). It was he who fixed the liturgical day of 19th March in 1479. Pope Innocent VIII, (1484 - 1492) and Pope Gregory XIII built on this until Pope Gregory XV (1621 - 1623) after the Council of Trent, declared 19th March the feast day of St. Joseph as a Holy day of obligation, with obligatory attendance at Mass and abstention from servile work (cf. *Indispensable Joseph I Know from the Pope*, Pg. 261). On December 8th, 1870, Pope Pius IX ordered that this feast be celebrated throughout the Church as a double of the first class. Holy Church also dedicates to St. Joseph the entire month of March. In addition, pious custom dedicates Wednesday of each week to the honour of St. Joseph. May 1st was established as the feast of St. Joseph the Worker by Pope Pius XII in 1955. The date was chosen to coincide with the date on which Labour Day is observed in many countries. His intention was to elevate and sanctify the observance of Labour Day. Formerly, there was a solemnity of the Patronage of St. Joseph which was celebrated each year on the third Sunday after Easter, then changed to the Wednesday following the Second Sunday after Easter, with an octave following. On that day St. Joseph was honoured especially as the Spouse of the Blessed Virgin Mary and as Patron of the Universal Church.

Formerly, there was also a Feast of the Espousal of St. Joseph on January 23. In summary therefore, we have the following:-

(i)   23rd January - Holy Spouses, Mary and Joseph (Feast)
Celebrated by the Oblates of Saint Joseph

(ii)   19th March - Feast of Saint Joseph, Husband of Mary (Solemnity)

(iii) May 1st - Feast of Saint Joseph the Worker (Memorial)

(iv) December 30th or Sunday in the Octave of Christmas - Holy Family of Jesus, Mary and Joseph (Feast).

MARCH 19
SOLEMNITY OF ST. JOSEPH HUSBAND OF MARY

THE OFFICE OF THE READINGS

Invitatory
Lord, + open my lips.
And my mouth will proclaim your praise.

Ant: Come, let us worship Christ the Lord, as we honour the Blessed Virgin Mary and her spouse, Saint Joseph.

(The Antiphon is repeated after every stanza)

Psalm 100

Cry out with joy to the Lord, all the earth.
Serve the Lord with gladness.
Come before him, singing for joy.
Antiphon

Know that he, the Lord, is God.
He made us, we belong to him,
We are his people, the sheep of his flock.
Antiphon

Go within his gates, giving thanks.
Enter his courts with songs of praise.
Give thanks to him and bless his name.
Antiphon

Indeed, how good is the Lord,
Eternal his merciful love.
He is faithful from age to age.
Antiphon

Glory to the Father, and to the Son, and to the Holy Spirit:
As it was in the beginning, is now, and ever shall be world without end. Amen.
Antiphon

Hymn as at Morning Prayer

Ant 1: *The angel of the Lord appeared to Joseph, and said 'Joseph Son of David, do not be afraid to take Mary as your wife, she will give birth to a son and you must call his name Jesus'* (Alleluia)

PSALMODY   *Psalm 20(21):2-8, 14*

O Lord, your strength gives joy to the king
how your saving help makes him glad!
You have granted him his heart's desire;
you have not refused the prayer of his lips.

You came to meet him with the blessings of success, *
you have set on his head a crown of pure gold.

He asked you for life and this you have given, *
days that will last from age to age.

Your saving help has given him glory. *
You have laid upon him majesty and splendour,
you have granted your blessings to him for ever. *
You have made him rejoice with the joy of your
presence.

The king has put his trust in the Lord: *
through the mercy of the Most High he shall stand
firm.
O Lord, arise in your strength;
we shall sing and praise your power.

Glory be to the Father …. (To be repeated after
each Psalm)

Ant 1: *The angel of the lord appeared to Joseph, and said
'Joseph Son of David, do not be afraid to take Mary as your
wife, she will give birth to a son and you must call his name
Jesus'* (Alleluia)

Ant 2: *Joseph arose from his sleep and did what the angel of the
Lord had told him to do: he took Mary as his wife* (Alleluia)

It is good to give thanks to the Lord*
to make music to your name, O Most High,
to proclaim your love in the morning
and your truth in the watches of the night,
on the ten-stringed lyre and the lute, *
with the murmuring sound of the harp

Your deeds, O Lord, have made me glad; *
for the work of your hands I shout with joy.
O Lord, how great are your works! *
How deep are your designs!
The foolish man cannot know this
and the fool cannot understand.

Though the wicked spring up like grass *
and all who do evil thrive:
they are doomed to be eternally destroyed. *
But you, Lord, are eternally on high.

Ant 2: *Joseph arose from his sleep and did what the angel of the Lord had told him to do: he took Mary as his wife* (Alleluia)

Ant 3: *Joseph set out from Nazareth and went up to the city of David called Bethlehem to be registered with Mary* (Alleluia)

See how your enemies perish: *
all doers of evil are scattered.

To me you give the wild-ox's strength: *
you anoint me with the purest oil.
My eyes looked in triumph on my foes;
my ears heard gladly of their fall.

The just will flourish like the palm-tree
and grow like a Lebanon cedar.

Planted in the house of the Lord
they will flourish in the courts of our God,

still bearing fruit when they are old,
still full of sap, still green,
to proclaim that the Lord is just.
In him, my rock, there is no wrong.

Ant 3: *Joseph set out from Nazareth and went up to the city of David called Bethlehem to be registered with Mary* (Alleluia)

V. The virtuous man will bloom like a lily **(Alleluia)**

R. He will grow forever before the Lord **(Alleluia)**

THE FIRST READING

A READING FROM THE LETTER TO THE HEBREWS
Hebrew 11:1-16

Only faith can guarantee the blessings that we hope for; or prove the existence of the realities that at present remain unseen. It is for faith that our ancestors were commended. It is by faith that we understand that the world was created by one word from God, so that no apparent cause can account for the things that we can see. It was because of faith that Abel offered God a better sacrifice than Cain, and for that he was declared to be righteous when God made acknowledgement of his offerings. Though he is dead he still speaks only by faith. It was because of faith that Enoch was taken up and did not have to experience death: he was not to be found because God had taken him. This was because before his assumption it is attested that he had pleased God. Now it is impossible to please God without faith, since anyone who comes to him must believe that he exists and rewards those who try to find him. It was through his faith that Noah, when he had been warned by God of something that had never been seen before, felt a holy fear and built an ark to save his family. By his faith the world was convicted, and he was able to claim the righteousness which is the reward of faith. It was by faith that Abraham obeyed the call to set out for a country that was the inheritance given to him and his descendants, and that he set out without knowing where he was going. By faith he arrived, as a foreigner, in the Promised Land, and lived there as if in a strange country, with Isaac and Jacob, who were heirs with him of the same promise. They lived there in tents while he looked forward to a city founded, designed and built by God.

It was equally by faith that Sarah, in spite of being past the age, was made able to conceive, because she believed that he who had made the promise would be faithful to it. Because of this, there came from one man, and one who was already as good as dead himself, *more descendants than could be counted, as many as the stars of heaven or the grains of the sand on seashore.*

All these died in faith, before receiving any of the things that had been promised, but they saw them in the far distance and welcomed them, recognizing that they were only *strangers and nomads on earth.* People who use such terms about themselves make it quite plain that they are in search of their real homeland. They can hardly have meant the country they came from, since they had the opportunity to go back to it; but in fact they were longing for a better a homeland, their heavenly homeland. That is why God is not ashamed to be called their God, since he has founded the city for them.

R/ The word of the Lord

V/ Thanks be to God

Responsory *Rom 4:20, 22; Jas 2:22*

R/ No distrust made him waver concerning the promise of God but he grew strong in his faith as he gave glory to God. * that is why his faith was counted as righteousness **(Alleluia).**

V/ Faith and deeds worked together; his faith became perfect by what he did, * that is why his faith was counted as righteousness **(Alleluia)**

THE SECOND READING

Sermon 2, On Joseph

A reading from the sermon of Saint Bernadine of Siena

This is the general rule that applies to all individual graces given to a rational creature. Whenever divine grace selects someone to receive a particular grace, or some especially favoured position, all the gifts for his state are given to that person and enrich him abundantly. This is especially true of that Holy man Joseph, the supposed father of our Lord Jesus Christ; and true husband of the queen of the world and of the holy angels. He was chosen by the eternal father to be that faithful foster-parent and guardian of the most precious treasures of God, his Son and his spouse. This was the task which her so faithfully carried out. For this, the lord said to him, 'Good and faithful servant, enter into the joy of our land.' A comparison can be made between Joseph, and the whole church of Christ. Joseph was the specially chosen man through whom and under whom Christ entered the world fittingly and in an appropriate way. So, if the whole Church is in the debt of the Virgin Mary, since, through her it was able to receive the Christ, surely after her, it also owes to Joseph special thanks and veneration. For he it is who marks the closing of the Old Testament. In him the dignity of the prophets and the patriarchs achieves its promised fulfillment. Moreover, he alone possessed in the flesh what God in his goodness promised them over and again. It is beyond doubt that Christ did not deny to Joseph in heaven that intimacy, respect, and high honour which he showed to him as to a father during his own human life, but rather completed and perfected it. Justifiably the words of the Lord should be applied to him, 'Enter into the joy of your Lord.' Although it is the joy of eternal happiness that comes into the heart of man, the Lord prefers to say to him 'enter into joy'. The mystical implication is that this joy is not just made inside man, but surrounds him everywhere and absorbs him, as if he were plunged in an infinite abyss. Therefore be mindful of us, blessed Joseph, and intercede for us with him whom men thought to be your son. Win for us the favour of the most Blessed Virgin your spouse, the mother of him who lives and reigns with the Father and the Holy Spirit through ages unending. Amen.

R/ Lord you are merciful to us

V/ Thanks be to God

Responsory

R/. God has made me the father to the king and lord over his entire household; *he has lifted me up to preserve the lives of many **(Alleluia).**

V/. The lord has been my protector and helper; he has become my saviour; * he has lifted me up to preserve the lives of many **(Alleluia)**

TE DEUM

The concluding prayer as at Morning Prayer.

MORNING PRAYER

HYMN

Joseph, wise ruler of Gods earthly household,
Nearest of all men to the heart of Jesus,
Be still a father loving providing
For us, his brethren.
Saint strong and manly, chosen by the Father,
As trusted guardian of the Son eternal,

Guide us as once you guided wisdoms footsteps
With sure direction

Husband of Mary, loving and beloved,
Teach us the joy of love so pure and holy,
Warming our hearts with love for God's own
mother
By your example

Saint of today, blest with Mary's presence,
In death you rested in the arms of Jesus;
So at our ending, Jesus, Mary, Joseph,
Come to assist us

Ant 1: *The Shepherds came quickly and they found Mary and Joseph and the Child lying in the manger* (Alleluia)

A soul thirsting for God　　　　　*Psalm 62(63):2-9*

O God, you are my God, for you I long; *
for you my soul is thirsting.
My body pines for you*
like a dry, weary land without water
So, I gaze on you in the sanctuary*
to see your strength and your glory.

For your love is better than life,*
my lips will speak your praise.
So, I will bless you all my life, *
in your name I will lift up my hands
My soul shall be filled as with a banquet*

my mouth shall praise you with joy.

On my bed I remember you.*
On you I muse through the night
for you have been my help;*
in the shadow of your wings I rejoice.
My soul clings to you; *
your right hand holds me fast.

Glory be to the Father ....
Ant 1: *The Shepherds came quickly and they found Mary
and Joseph and the Child lying in the manger* (Alleluia)

Ant. 2: *Joseph and Mary, the mother of Jesus, marvelled at
what was being said of him, and Simeon gave them his blessing*
(Alleluia)

Let every creature praise the Lord,
Canticle. *Dan. 3:57-88. 56*

O all you works of the Lord, O bless the Lord. *
To him be highest glory and praise for ever.

And you, angels of the Lord, O bless the Lord. *
To him be highest glory and praise for ever

And you, the heavens of the Lord, O bless the Lord. *
And you, clouds of the sky, O bless the Lord.
And you, all armies of the Lord, O bless the Lord. *
To him be highest glory and praise for ever.
And you, sun and moon, O bless the Lord. *
And you, the stars of the heavens, O bless the Lord

And you, showers and rain, O bless the Lord. *
To him be highest glory and praise for ever

And you, all you breezes and winds, O bless the Lord. *
And you, fire and heat, O bless the Lord.
And you, cold and heat, O bless the Lord. *
To him be highest glory and praise for ever.

And you, showers and dew, O bless the Lord. *
And you, frosts and cold, O bless the Lord.
And you, frost and snow, O bless the Lord. *
To him be highest glory and praise for ever.

And you, night-time and day, O bless the Lord. *
And you, darkness and light, O bless the Lord.
And you, lightning and clouds, O bless the Lord. *
To him be highest glory and praise for ever.

O let the earth bless the Lord. *
To him be highest glory and praise for ever.
And you, mountains and hills, O bless the Lord. *
And you, all plants of the earth, O bless the Lord.
And you, fountains and springs, O bless the Lord. *
To him be highest glory and praise for ever.

And you, rivers and seas, O bless the Lord. *
And you, creatures of the sea, O bless the Lord.
And you, every bird in the sky, O bless the Lord. +
And you, wild beasts and tame, O bless the Lord.
To him be highest glory and praise for ever.

And you, children of men, O bless the Lord. *
To him be highest glory and praise for ever.
O Israel, bless the Lord. O bless the Lord. *
And you, priests of the Lord, O bless the Lord.
And you, servants of the Lord, O bless the Lord. *
To him be highest glory and praise for ever.

And you, spirits and souls of the just, O bless the Lord. *
And you, holy and humble of heart, O bless the Lord.
Ananias, Azarias, Mizael, O bless the Lord. *
To him be highest glory and praise for ever.

Let us praise the Father, the Son, and Holy Spirit. *
To you be highest glory and praise for ever.
May you be blessed, O Lord, in the heavens. *
To you be highest glory and praise for ever

The Glory be is not said after this Canticle, as it contains a doxology.

Ant. 2: *Joseph and Mary, the mother of Jesus, marvelled at what was being said of him, and Simeon gave them his blessing* (Alleluia)

Ant. 3: *Joseph arose from sleep and, taking the child and his mother with him, left that night for Egypt, where he stayed until the death of Herod* (Alleluia)

The song of joy of the saints *Psalm 149*

Sing a new song to the Lord, *

his praise in the assembly of the faithful
Let Israel rejoice in its Maker, *
Let Sion's sons exult in their king.
Let them praise his name with dancing *
and make music with tumbrel and harp

For the Lord takes delight in his people. *
He crowns the poor with salvation.
Let the faithful rejoice in their glory, *
shout for joy and take their rest.
Let the praise of God be on their lips*
and a two-edged sword in their hand,

to deal out vengeance to the nations*
and punishment on all the peoples
to bind their kings in chains*
and their nobles in fetters of iron;
to carry out the sentence pre-ordained: *
this honour is for all his faithful.

Glory be to the Father ....

Ant. 3: *Joseph arose from sleep and, taking the child and his mother with him, left that night for Egypt, where he stayed until the death of Herod* (Alleluia)

SCRIPTURE READING

2 Sam 7:28-29

Lord you are God indeed, your words are true and you have made this fair promise to your servant. Be pleased, then, to bless the house of your servant, that it may continue forever in your presence; for you, Lord God, have spoken; and with your blessing the house of your servant will be forever blessed.

Short Responsory

R/. The lord made him master of his house. **Repeat R/.**

V/. He constituted him ruler of all the possessed. **R/.**

V/. Glory be to the Father…. **R/.**

Eastertide

R/. The lord made him master of his house, alleluia, alleluia. **Repeat R/.**

V/. He constituted him ruler of all he possessed. **R/.**

V/. Glory be to the Father…. **R/.**

Benedictus Ant. Joseph settled in a town called Nazareth. This was to fulfil the words spoken about Christ by the prophets: he will be called a Nazarene **(Alleluia).**

Intercessions

Whatever we do or say let us do it in the name of the

Lord Jesus, giving thanks to God the Father through him. **R/. Lord hear us.**

As Joseph believed what you had told him, and became the guardian of your Son: so may we put our faith in you, and receive the fulfilment of your promise. **R/.**

Father give us that faith which gives substance to our hopes, and make us certain of realities we do not see. **R/.**

Joseph took the child Jesus into his care, loving and accepting him as his own: may we accept all that God gives us, and care for those entrusted to us. **R/.**

You have given man authority over the work of your hands and invited him to share in your creation: help us to accept the responsibility by working for your glory and for the good of all mankind. **R/.**

Concluding Prayer

Almighty God, at the beginning of our salvation, when Mary conceived your Son and brought him forth into the world, you placed them under Joseph's watchful care. May his prayer still help your Church to be an equally faithful guardian of your mysteries, and a sign of Christ to mankind. We make our prayer through Jesus Christ our lord. Amen.

The Lord bless us, keep us from every evil and bring us to life everlasting. Amen!

MEETING OF A SOCIETY OF ST. JOSEPH

Before or Around a Statue of St. Joseph

1. Opening Hymn: In the name of the Father, and of the Son, and of the Holy Spirit. Amen.

    Invocation of the Holy Spirit

V: Come Holy Spirit, fill the Heart of the faithful

R: And enkindle in us the fire of thy love

V: Send forth thy spirit and they shall be created

R: And thou shall renew the face of the Earth

Let us pray: O God, who by the light of the Holy Spirit didst' instruct the hearts of the faithful, grant that by the same spirit, we may be truly wise and ever rejoice in his divine consolation through the same Christ our Lord.

V: Thou, O Lord will open our lips

R: And our tongue shall announce thy praise

V: Incline unto our aid O Lord

R: O Lord, make haste to help us

V: Glory be to the Father, etc.

R: As it was in the beginning etc.

2. St. Joseph Rosary

3. Litany of St. Joseph

4. Scripture Reading and meditation on the Gospel of the coming Sunday

5. Reflection or Sharing on the Gospel

6. Intercessory prayers (For the Church, the Nation, Families, Workers, Unemployed, Vocation, for Spouses, Singles and other intentions)

7. Offering (for the poor)

8. Closing Prayer

9. Closing Hymn in Honour of St. Joseph

HYMNS

1. HAIL HOLY JOSEPH

1. Hail, holy Joseph, Hail,
   Chaste Spouse of Mary, hail
   Pure as the lily flower
   In Eden's peaceful vale.

2. Hail, holy Joseph, hail!
   Father of Christ esteemed,
   Father be thou to those
   Thy precious Son redeemed.

3. Hail, holy Joseph, hail,
   Prince of the house of God
   May His best graces be
   By the sweet hands bestowed.

4. Hail, holy Joseph, hail,
   Comrade of angels, hail
   Cheer thou the hearts that faint,
   And guide the steps that fail.

5. Hail, holy Joseph, hail!
   God's choice were thou alone.
   To thee the Word made flesh
   Was subject as a son.

6. Mother of Jesus, bless,
   And bless, ye Saints on high,
   All meek and simple Souls
   That to Saint Joseph Cry.

2.   O BLESSED SAINT JOSEPH

1.   O blessed Saint Joseph how great was thy worth,
The one chosen shadow of God upon earth
Called Father of Jesus, ah, then wilt thou be
Sweet Spouse or Our Lady! A father to me

2.   For thou to the pilgrim art father and guide
And Jesus and Mary felt safe by thy side;
Ah blessed Saint Joseph how safe should I be,
Sweet Spouse of Our Lady! If thou were with me.

3.   When the treasures of God were unsheltered on earth,
Safe Keeping was found for them both in thy worth
O Father of Jesus, be father to me
Sweet spouse of our Lady we hasten to thee.

3.   DEAR GUARDIAN OF MARY

(Novena final Hymn)

1.   Dear Guardian of Mary! Dear Nurse of Her Child!
Life's ways are full weary, the desert is wild,
Bleak sands are all 'round us, no home can we see;
Sweet Spouse of Our Lady, we lean safe on thee.

2.   God chose thee for Jesus and Mary -wilt thou
Forgive a poor exile for choosing thee now
There's no Saint in Heaven, St. Joseph like thee.
Sweet Spouse of Our Lady! Do thou plead for me.

3.   O Blessed St. Joseph, how great was thy worth
The one chosen image of God upon earth
The father of Jesus, ah then wilt thou be,
Chaste spouse of our Lady, a father to me.

4. SING OF MARY, SING OF JOSEPH

1.   Sing of Mary, pure and lowly,
Virgin Mother undefiled
Sing of God's own Son most holy
Who became her little child.
Fairest Child of fairest mother,
God the Lord who came to earth,
Word made flesh, our very brother
Takes our nature by his birth.

2.   Sing of Joseph, nurturing father,
To the incarnate Son of God.
Loving husband for God's mother
As towards David's town they plod
Filled with justice, strength and wisdom,
Joseph was their rock and guide.
Now he guards God's pilgrim people,
Steadfast patron at our side.

3.   Glory be to God the Father
Glory be to God the Son,
Glory be to God the Spirit
Glory to the Three in One.
Hear the hearts of Joseph, Mary,
And all saints the hymn intone,
While the church, God's earthly family,
Echoes praise to heaven's throne.

5. GREAT ST. JOSEPH

1. Great St. Joseph, son of David,
    Spouse of Mary undefiled;
    Guardian of the Holy Family,
    Father of the Holy Child.
    God presented thee with blessings,
    Glorified thy life obscure;
    Made thee guardian of all virgins,
    Consolation of the poor.

2. Ornament of life domestic,
    Model for the toiler's day;
    Hope of all the sick and weary,
    In the hour of death our stay.
    Great protector universal
    Of the Church, we thee acclaim.
    Hear our prayers, O great St. Joseph,
    When we call upon thy name.

3. Clasped in Jesus' arms and Mary's,
    When death gently came at last,
    Thy pure spirit sweetly sighing,
    From its earthly dwelling passed.
    Great St. Joseph, by thy passing,
    May our death be like thine.
    And with Jesus, Mary, Joseph,
    May our souls forever shine.

6. JOSEPH THE SCRIPTURES LOVE TO TRACE

(Tune of Cath. Hymn Book 1)

1. Joseph, the scriptures love to trace
   The glories of thy kingly line
   Yet no succession of thy race
   No long posterity was thine.

2. Of her the everlasting spouse
   Who must a virgin ever be
   The faithful ruler of his house
   Who owns no fatherhood in thee.

3. There were no songs of old renown
   No crowds to greet you when you came
   Two wanderers, to your native town
   That lost inheritance to claim.

4. But hard the hearts, and old cold the air
   And mean the lodging where you lay
   And long the exile you must bear
   Till upstart Herod's dying day.

5. And though thy Son were God indeed
   Over that home no angels sang
   But still, through years of toil and need
   Hammer and mallet bravely sang.

6. And surely t'was a gracious thing
   When, standing at his father's knee,

The world's great craftsman and its king
Not king but craftsman learned to be.

7. FRIEND OF THE ANGELS IN PARADISE STILL
(Tune of: Abide With Me)

1. Friend of the Angels in paradise still,
   Helpless humanity's refuge from ill,
   Joseph, the worship and strength of our days
   Graciously hear us who sing thy praise.

2. Chosen thou were by the makers decree
   Spotless virginity's bridegroom to be;
   Thee the eternal His father would call,
   Steward on each of His bounty to all.

3. Housed with the oxen he lay in the cold
   Kings had but dreamed of it, prophets foretold
   Thou thy redeemer rejoicing didst see,
   Father and worshipper, bending the knee.

4. Monarch of monarchs, whom worlds must obey
   Hell doth acknowledge him, bowed to his sway
   Heaven in its course his word doth fulfil
   He became subject on earth to thy will.

5. Glory to God, three in one, let us own
   Who mid the angels thy merits doth crown
   Would but he grant, through those merits
   That we live everlasting, Joseph with thee

8. LOOK DOWN TO US, ST. JOSEPH

1. Look down to us, Saint Joseph,
   Protector of our Lord,
   Who followed you through deserts,
   And gave you blessed reward,
   Our foes are yet about us.
   Be strength now at our side,
   Be light against the darkness,
   Saint Joseph, be our guide!

2. We venerate your Justice,
   The gospels praise your name,
   You are the saint all humble,
   Who gained eternal fame;
   In your devoted family
   Our souls in trust confide,
   Direct our way to heaven,
   Saint Joseph, be our guide.

9. LET'S SING THE NAME OF JOSEPH

1. Let's sing the name of Joseph,
   The Father's image on earth
   To him the Lord confided
   His gems of precious worth
   The Son of the Eternal,
   The Virgin Mother of God
   Most privilege of fathers
   That e'er this earth has trod (2X)

2. We praise thee, blest ST. Joseph,
   The perfect model of men

The weary workman's sunshine
That brings him joy again
How great if we are chosen,
Another Joseph to be
To work for Christ in silence
And true humility (2X)

10.   O SAINT JOSEPH

1.   Once I have seen a child in a manger
Sleeping in peace embraced by a mother
And there stood a man of great patience
Watching still the child humble and mild

O St. Joseph humble and mild

You gave yourself to comfort me and the child

2.   Angels from high singing their praises
Shepherds awakened by heavenly voices
Come and see the child in his little manger,
Giving gifts of love, proclaim Him divine.

APPRECIATION

Our appreciation goes to the Most Holy Trinity and the inspirations of St. Joseph and the Blessed Virgin Mary who guided us through the process of putting this prayer book together. We appreciate authors of books (especially Fr. Larry Toschi, OSJ) and internet sites that provided us with some helpful materials. The Director of the Pius Union of St. Luigi Guanella in Rome was especially gracious to allow us translate and use some prayers from their manual of prayer booklet titled *Tempi con San Giuseppe* (Times with St, Joseph) to serve our purpose. With grateful heart we also appreciate all the Treasures, especially Esther Ezeigbo, Sr. Celine Onafowope, OSF Nancy Samuel-Inyang, Sir Ted Ngu, Fr. Bonaventure Ashibi, OSJ, Fr. Patrick Adejumo, OSJ, Fr. Anthony Okem, OSJ and Fr. Dennis Ujomu, OSJ who by their collaboration, suggestions and proofreading of the manual made this project a reality. Your love for St. Joseph and the assistance given are indeed invaluable and have contributed to the success of this book. May the Lord bless and reward you all. Amen! In a special way, we thank the Provincial Superior of Our Lady Queen of Nigeria Province of the Oblates of St. Joseph, Fr. Paul Agabo, OSJ, for his approval of this manual of prayer. We appreciate also the encouragement and support of our Superior General Fr. Jan Pelczarski, OSJ, and the members of his General Council.

We wish to make known that the intention of this book is to facilitate the promotion of devotion to our spiritual father St. Joseph and not for any particular material profit or interest. So, kindly help to make it known to all who seek to serve the interest of Jesus through the imitation of St. Joseph. Be sure to have others in mind as you get a copy for yourself!

www.ingramcontent.com/pod-product-compliance
Lightning Source LLC
Chambersburg PA
CBHW051828150726
47998CB00001B/333